THE FUTURE SHAPE OF
ANGLICAN MINISTRY

THE FUTURE SHAPE OF
ANGLICAN MINISTRY

Edited by Donald M. Lewis

REGENT COLLEGE PUBLISHING
Vancouver, British Columbia

The Future Shape of Anglican Ministry
Copyright © 2004 Regent College Publishing
All rights reserved.

Published 2004 by Regent College Publishing
5800 University Boulevard, Vancouver, BC V6T 2E4 Canada
www.regentpublishing.com

National Library of Canada Cataloguing in Publication Data

The future shape of Anglican ministry / edited by Donald M. Lewis.

Includes bibliographical references.
ISBN 1-57383-307-X

   1. Pastoral theology—Anglican Communion. 2. Anglican
Communion—Clergy. I. Lewis, Donald Munro, 1950–

BX5175.F87 2004   253   C2004-901919

CONTENTS

5

SECTION TWO: SERMONS

SECTION THREE: SEMINARS

CONTRIBUTORS

Archdeacon Lydia Constant up in Opaskwa Cree Nation. In the 1980s, she started studying TEE courses at Henry Budd College for Ministry in The Pas, Manitoba, supplemented by courses at Vancouver School of Theology and Cook College and Theological School (Tempe, AZ). She received the Diploma in Theology from Henry Budd College in 1990, and the extension MDiv degree from VST in 1999. She was ordained Deacon in 1988 (Diocese of Brandon), Priest in 1990, and appointed Archdeacon for Indigenous Ministries in 1994. She has been a part-time instructor at Henry Budd College since 1988, and is involved in all aspects of formation for indigenous ministry.

Dr. George Egerton has taught in the History Department of the University of British Columbia since the early 1970s and specializes in international relations. He has served as General Synod delegate from the Diocese of New Westminster, having been elected to this position four times. He also served on the Long Range Planning Committee of the Anglican Church of Canada. George and his wife, Manya, are the Western editors of *InCourage,* a publication produced by Barnabas Anglican Ministries.

Archbishop Reginald Hollis received his basic theological training at Cambridge University in England and at McGill University in Montreal. He was ordained as a priest in 1956 and served in parochial ministry in Montreal until 1974 when he was elected Bishop of Montreal. He was later elected Archbishop of the Ecclesiastical Province of Canada. In 1990 he resigned to become the Episcopal Director of the Anglican Fellowship of Prayer based in Orlando, Florida. He is now retired from full-time ministry and lives in Victoria, BC.

Bishop Victoria Matthews grew up in Toronto where she attended school and university. Further studies included Yale Divinity School in the Master of Divinity program. Bishop Matthews graduated, was ordained in the Diocese of Toronto in 1979, and spent the next several years in parish ministry. Elected Suffragan Bishop of Toronto in 1993, she was consecrated in February 1994. In 1997 she was elected Diocesan Bishop of Edmonton. In addition to her diocesan responsibilities, Bishop Matthews is a Trustee of Yale University and chair of the Primate's Theological Commission.

Archbishop Thomas O. Morgan was raised on a farm in Saskatchewan, and served all of his ministry in rural multi-point parishes. He studied at the University of Saskatchewan, and at King's College, London. He was ordained to the priesthood in 1966, in Blackburn, Lancashire, where he served a three-year curacy, before returning to Canada. He was elected Bishop of Saskatchewan in 1985, serving eight years, then was elected Bishop of Saskatoon in 1993. In 2000 he was elected Archbishop of the Ecclesiastical Province of Rupert's Land. He retired in 2003. He has two sons and a daughter, and four grandchildren. His wife, Lillian, is a Registered Nurse, serving in the Sherbrooke Community Centre in Saskatoon.

Rev. Prof. J. I. Packer is the Board of Governors' Professor of Systematic Theology at Regent College. Born in England, he did his undergraduate training at Oxford University before going on to do doctoral studies at the same university. Ordained in England, he served for a time as a principal of an Anglican theological college. He is best known as an author and speaker, being one of the most widely read Anglican theologians in the world today.

Rev. Dr. Barry Parker was educated at the University of Western Ontario and completed a Master of Divinity degree at Huron College in 1986 and a Doctor of Ministry from Fuller Seminary. Following his ordination he served as rector of All Saints Anglican Church in Drayton Valley, Alberta (1986-91) and then as rector of St. John the Evangelist in Edmonton (1991-97). He is currently the rector of one of Canada's largest Anglican churches, St. Paul's Bloor Street, in Toronto.

Rev. Canon Harold Percy was educated at York University and at Wycliffe College, Toronto. He is the former director of the Institute of Evangelism at Wycliffe. He is currently the Rector of Holy Trinity, Streetsville, Ontario. Harold is well-known for his expertise in evangelism and writes a regular column on the subject in the *Anglican Journal*. He continues to serve the Institute of Evangelism as a Consulting Director and is Adjunct Lecturer in Evangelism at Wycliffe College.

Rev. Dr. Harry S. D. Robinson is the Chaplain of the Anglican Studies program at Regent College. Born in Ontario, he trained at the University of Toronto and at the London College of Divinity. Ordained in the Diocese of Toronto, he served as the rector of Little Trinity Church in Toronto, before becoming rector of St. John's Shaughnessy Anglican Church in Vancouver. He retired in 1993. He is well-known as a preacher and a missioner.

Rev. David Short was born to missionary parents in East Africa. His family returned to Sydney, Australia where his father served as the Bishop of North Sydney. He was trained at the University of New South Wales and then at Moore College in Sydney, an Anglican seminary. David originally came to Canada to pursue a Master of Theology at Regent College and while he was here was appointed as the rector of St. John's Shaughnessy Anglican Church.

Rev. Dr. George Sumner is Principal of Wycliffe College, an Anglican theological college affiliated with the University of Toronto. He was born in the United States and did his undergraduate studies at Harvard University and his Master of Divinity and PhD work at Yale Divinity College and at Yale University in New Haven, Connecticut. Following his ordination he served as a missionary in Africa. His research interests include Christology, inculturation and the theology of missions.

Bishop Christopher Williams was born in Cheshire in England, educated at the University of Manchester and received his theological training at Cranmer Hall, University of Durham. He is married to a Scottish wife and they have two adult children. He was ordained deacon in England in 1960 and immediately went to the Canadian Arctic where he was priested (1962) and served in Coppermine (now Kugluktuk), then in Spence Bay (Taloyoak), Frobisher Bay (Iqaluit), Sugluk (Salluit) from 1961-1972, followed by placements in Cape Dorset, Baker Lake, and then for ten years in Yellowknife. He was elected Suffragan Bishop of the Arctic in 1987, Coadjutor Bishop in 1990 and diocesan in 1991. He retired in 2001.

INTRODUCTION

The Anglican Communion faces many challenges in the opening years of the twenty-first century. This volume seeks to examine those challenges and to consider the shape of Anglican ministry in this new millennium. Clearly old patterns are changing and our notions of Anglican normalcy are being overthrown. A Church that has long prided itself on its reverence for Scripture, Tradition and Reason is having to rethink its relation to the world and to its inherited doctrines and certainties in ways that our forbears perhaps never did.

The chapters of this book were, in the first instance, presented at a conference entitled "The Future Shape of Anglican Ministry" that was held at Regent College in Vancouver in May 2000. This conference was sponsored by the Anglican Studies Program at Regent College and attended by approximately 150 people from across Canada and the United States. It was followed up by a similar conference in 2002 at Wycliffe College in Toronto which was jointly sponsored by Wycliffe and Regent, and another conference at Regent in May 2005. [For those interested in Regent's Anglican Studies program, please feel free to visit our webpage (www.RegentAnglicanStudies.org).]

The conference from which this book emerged was designed to assist those considering Anglican ordination and to help them to answer the questions that concern many prospective ordinands: Am I called to ordained ministry? How can I be certain of this? What does ordained ministry involve? What might it require of me? Of my spouse? Of my family? Should I consider moving forward with a church that seems so fraught with difficulty and division? How is one best trained for ordained ministry? Are there new forms of ministry that I might be better suited to than the traditional clergy role? And so the list goes on.

The material in the book is organized into three sections. In the first, there are six "big picture" essays that examine some of these questions. Dr. George Egerton, a member of the University of British Columbia's history faculty has been an active layman in the Anglican Church of Canada, having served as a member of General Synod and as a member of the Synod's Long-Range Planning Committee. His analysis of the state of global Anglicanism was written in 2000, but his foresight has proved 20/20 and his critique penetrating.

George Sumner is the Principal of Wycliffe College in Toronto, Canada's largest Anglican theological school. His insights into the future of ordained Anglican ministry will be helpful to those pondering the possibility of ordination. Victoria Matthews, the Bishop of Edmonton, has very helpful suggestions for those thinking about how they might best prepare themselves for pastoral ministry. Barry Parker, rector of St. Paul's (Bloor Street) in Toronto, offers a helpful retrospective on his own baptism into ministry.

The other two contributions in this section have been made by my friend and colleague, Dr. J. I. Packer, the Board of Governors Professor of Theology at Regent College and the director of Regent College's Anglican Studies Program. His two essays are much expanded from the talks he gave in 2000 and are worth the price of this volume alone. In my view should be required reading for every ordinand and would probably be of immeasurable help to many clergy (both Anglican and non-Anglican) as well.

INTRODUCTION

The second section includes two sermons given at the conference by two of Canada's most effective Anglican pastors and preachers. The Rev. Dr. Harry Robinson is a legend in Canadian Anglicanism and I hope that the transcription of his sermon will give readers some sense of the remarkable and creative approach to preaching that has long characterized his ministry. The other sermon is by David Short, Harry's successor as the rector of St. John's Anglican Church in Vancouver.

The final section presents the wisdom shared in the seminars at the conference. These (often brief) offerings address specific concerns of different sorts of ordinands: Am I suited to rural ministry? What about ministry in an aboriginal community? What skill sets are needed? What about starting out in ministry? How can I maximize my time in training for ministry? And, of course, the vexed question of discovering my vocation. The authors are a veritable who's who of Canadian Anglicanism, and include no less than two archbishops, a bishop, an archdeacon, two professors of theology, and one of Canada's most gifted Anglican evangelists.

It is hoped that these contributions will continue to nurture and build up those whom God is calling to Gospel ministry in the Anglican communion.

Donald M. Lewis, D.Phil. (Oxon.)
Professor, Church History
Secretary, Anglican Studies Program
Regent College, Vancouver

SECTION ONE:
ESSAYS

CHAPTER 1

THE FUTURE OF WORLD ANGLICANISM

George Egerton

I speak as a product of World Anglicanism, whose ancestors were all members of the Church of Ireland before coming to Canada at the beginning of the last century. Somehow they all lost the Anglican connection in the new country and became Presbyterians, Methodists, Pentecostals and "nothings." Raised as a Pentecostal, I came to faith as a graduate student studying in London when I was captivated by the preaching of John Stott and the worship and community of All Souls, Langham Place.

I speak, as well, as an historian, primarily of modern international relations, but currently engaged in studying the changing relations between politics and religion in Canada since the Second World War.

Finally, I speak as a long-time participant and observer in Canadian Anglicanism: serving on the General Synod and its former Long-Range Planning Committee, a member of Barnabas Anglican Ministries, co-editor of BAM's journal *InCourage*, a member (from the beginning) of the Essentials partnership, editor of *Anglican*

Essentials[1] (a publication of the addresses given at the Essentials '94 conference in Montreal) and, finally, a church school teacher at St. Philip's (Dunbar) for twenty-eight years.

What Future for World Anglicanism? At first glance, the future for Anglicanism, especially in the First World, might seem bleak and uncertain. Statistics on religious demography show that all the churches of First World Anglicanism (FWA) have declined radically in membership and participation since the 1960s. Within this time frame the Episcopal Church of the United States of America (ECUSA) has lost more than one-third of its membership. Sociologist Reginald Bibby predicted in 1993 that numerical trends indicated that within twenty-five years, Canada's United and Anglican Churches "may well be almost decimated."[2]

The dominant response of FWA to the challenges of late modernity has been cultural accommodation and theological revisionism, with the ironic result not of regained salience, but rather cultural marginalization.

Episcopal delinquency by a minority of revisionist FWA bishops, who are generally championed by the popular media, has resulted in departures from Scriptural authority, sacramental tradition, the historic creeds and episcopal responsibility and unity—indeed, departures from all the elements of the Chicago-Lambeth Quadrilateral (the defining principles of World Anglicanism). These departures have done great harm to a central distinctive of Anglicanism: episcopal leadership, where bishops, at their consecration, profess and promise—in the words of the Prayer Book—"to hold and maintain the Doctrine, Sacraments, and Discipline of Christ, as the Lord hath commanded in his holy Word."

We see, then, deep divisions in FWA churches, with schism a very real and imminent danger in several of them, especially the ECUSA. There is in FWA great confusion over theology, belief and identity, with little agreement over what should be taught to members and their children, let alone the unchurched. Most of the theological colleges and seminaries are wastelands of mediocrity, special causes and therapies; few of them serve their church constituencies in the vital mission of forming and preparing new leadership.

Such churches have ceased to function as the conscience of their nations or address the rising moral anomie of First World peoples, whose cultures are steeped in individualism, consumerism and sexual permissiveness. A recent poll conducted for the *New York Times* tells us that the highest value popularly embraced by Americans is the right to chose our own values and behaviour: "No strong God. No strong rules. No strong superiors, moral or otherwise." The Way We Live Now poll finds that most Americans want to decide for themselves "what is right, good and meaningful."[3] Well, what's new? The primordial sin presented in the creation narrative was defiance of God in eating the fruit of the tree of the knowledge of good and evil. In modern cultures of narcissism and permissiveness, the mainline churches have ceased to offer any distinct moral compass. As a result they share in the general moral anomie.

A final item of bad news can be cited. We are told that the Anglican Church of Canada faces financial ruin at the national level as the accumulating claims from aboriginal lawsuits over abuse suffered in church-run schools surpass the assets of the National Church. I am persuaded that something more than rightful apology and restitution for real abuse is at work here. What we are seeing is a political culture and jurisprudence that wishes to stigmatize all Christian religion in its public functions as culturally abusive.

SIGNS OF HOPE

Enough bad news. Although the themes and issues identified in what I have said are often given primacy in the popular media, thank God this is not the full story. What reasons are there for hope—especially for those contemplating ordained ministry? In what follows, I will attempt to identify and expand upon themes, trends and changes that, indeed, give good cause for hope.

Reaffirming Essentials

First, let me say I am more hopeful for the future of Anglicanism than I was ten or fifteen years ago when observation and participation in national and diocesan structures often brought despair. In 1987 the then Bishop of New Westminster, Douglas Hambidge, asked me to chair a Diocesan Commission on Levels of Ministry (CLOM). After more than a year of broad-ranging consultation on what was wrong and how to fix it, as well as opportunities for new ministry, I presented our report to the Diocesan Synod in May of 1989. Here is the opening section of our recommendations:

> In attempting to understand and respond theologically to the challenges of modern Canadian culture, the Anglican church, along with other "mainline" denominations, has experienced several decades of controversial change, as old rites, traditions, doctrines, mores, and habits have been altered or abandoned, while new patterns of belief, worship, and mission have struggled for acceptance. Since the 1960s, when we were called to leave the "Comfortable Pew," an array of theologians have invited the attention and engagement of the churches. Much has been learned from this theological discourse about how churches can attempt to remain relevant in modern culture. Over time, however, the more radical theological agenda has combined with cultural pressures to force questioning of central Christian beliefs and ethics. The result has been increasing controversy and division within the leadership of Canada's leading denominations, and mounting confusion in the pew. In the Anglican Church, theological conflict has been comparatively muted and civil, as our energies have been largely absorbed in liturgical reform. There is nevertheless much evidence that we are deeply divided and confused on many matters of theology, that Anglican identity has been seriously eroded, and that our mission has lost focus in face of a plethora of urgent causes placed on our national and Diocesan agendas. It would seem that our church needs a time of rediscovering and reaffirming the essentials of our faith as Christians, and our identity as Anglicans. This does

not mean that we would cease to be in dialogue with modern culture, nor closed to new wisdom from whatever source; it would entail a more critical approach in discourse with the dominant ideologies and value systems of modernity, a more assertive presentation of Christian essentials, and the avoidance of excessive accommodation and assimilation. Such a reaffirmation and reassertion of Christian essentials seems necessary if we are to see revitalization of Anglican ministry.[4]

The Report was received by the Diocesan leadership with extreme reserve, cold silence and aversion; nothing was done to affirm its principal recommendations beyond hiring a congregational development officer. Similar analyses and recommendations contributed throughout my participation for almost a decade on the Long-Range Planning Committee of General Synod met with similar responses. When a new bishop was elected in New Westminster, his agenda was, to put it mildly, unsympathetic to reaffirmation and reassertion of Christian essentials. All of this was cause for some discouragement.

What I could not see clearly at the time was that my efforts in the Long-Range Planning Committee and the theological recommendations of CLOM were a small local expression of a gathering movement of evangelical, charismatic and Catholic reaffirmation and re-articulation of Christian orthodoxy, a movement that would have vast import for the cause of Christ locally, nationally, internationally and ecumenically—sometimes outside and beyond the official structures and elites of the churches, but also ultimately within these structures. Here I can but mention briefly what I summarized in editing *Anglican Essentials*.

In contrast with the liberal Protestant and liberationist Catholic agendas, the conservative and neo-orthodox response to the crisis of the churches in modernity has come from the Papacy, the "non-Christendom" Protestant churches and the growing evangelical and charismatic movements within the former Christendom churches, along with their burgeoning Third World adherents. Following are

21

some of the salient themes of conservative theological and strategic responses.

- the reassertion of Papal authority for Catholics in the wake of the discourse and pronouncements generated by Vatican II (1962–65), in such encyclicals as *Humanae Vitae* (1968); the defense of traditional Catholicism through such movements and organizations as Opus Dei; the Papal leadership of John Paul II in affirmation of the social mission of the church in struggles for economic justice and human rights, while restating traditional doctrine on such issues as the priesthood, divorce, abortion, birth control, sexual morality, gender roles and homosexual behaviour—encoded now in the new *Catechism of the Catholic Church*[5] and communicated in such leading Papal encyclicals as *Veritatis Splendor* (1993), *Evangelium Vitae* (1995) and *Fides et Ratio* (1998).

- the resurgence of evangelical Protestantism nationally in inter-denominational alliances (e.g., The Evangelical Fellowship of Canada became the most effective religious lobby by the mid-1980s) and internationally in the World Evangelical Fellowship, with the renewal of theology and mission signified by the International Congress on World Evangelization (Lausanne, 1974) and the publication of the *Lausanne Covenant* (1975) and the *Willowbank Report: Christ and Culture* (1978), which reaffirmed Reformational Protestant themes on the authority of Scripture, traditional teaching on personal morality, while inviting greater cultural and social engagement as part of a renewed international mission of evangelization

- the development of the charismatic movement beyond classic Pentecostalism, first in American Episcopal and Catholic circles in the 1960s, but spreading powerfully—internationally and denominationally—with its emphasis on spiritual renewal and expression; today it constitutes an emergent new force in World Christianity.

- the emergence of a "new religious right" in American politics in the 1970s and '80s, dedicated to traditional Christian personal and family values and neo-conservative economics and skillful in exploiting the medium of television.

- the renewal of evangelical Anglican theology and mission heralded in Britain by the Keele '67 Congress with its *National Evangelical Anglican Congress Statement* (1967) and *Guidelines: Anglican Evangelicals Face the Future* (1967), followed by the Nottingham Congress of 1977.

- the national roles undertaken in Canada by the Prayer Book Society, Anglican Renewal Ministries and Barnabas Anglican Ministries, who joined to plan and organize Essentials '94.

Indeed, Essentials '94 was a sign and rich source of hope—personal hope, hope for the members of the cooperating organizations and hope for the church that we love.

Lambeth '98

Lambeth '98 stands as perhaps the most important of the thirteen Lambeth Conferences. With its overwhelming reaffirmation of scriptural authority and traditional sexual teaching, while rejecting homosexual practice as contrary to Scripture, the Lambeth resolutions were welcomed warmly by conservatives and furiously denounced by leading liberal bishops and commentators. The passionate nature of the liberal rejections and denials, together with the decisive nature of the voting, indicate that the Lambeth decisions mark a watershed in the history of World Anglicanism.

The voice of Lambeth, of course, offers new hope and encouragement to orthodox, faithful Anglicans—particularly in the First World Churches. What are some of the signs of hope we can see and infer from the Lambeth Conference?

First we can note the witness and role of the Two-Thirds World bishops as exemplars of theological leadership, many with academic doctorates; exemplars of evangelism with burgeoning national churches; and exemplars of courage, many of whose churches face deadly persecution. The enhanced leadership of Anglican bishops from Africa, Asia and South America is reflective of the larger demographic shifting of Christianity, including Anglicanism, to the Two-Thirds World in the latter half of the twentieth century. In 1900 more than 80 percent of the world's Christians were located in Europe and North America; by 2000 the non-Western world contained more than 60 percent of the Christian total.[6] Indeed, it is estimated now that on any given Sunday there are more Anglican worshipers in Uganda than in all of Britain, Europe and North America combined. First World Anglican membership represents less than 40 percent of the c. 70 million World Anglican Communion.[7]

Lambeth also heralded a welcome reassertion of episcopal vocation, integrity and unity, as episcopal majorities from First World Churches joined Two-Thirds World bishops in the decisive votes. The Archbishop of Canterbury, in his opening Presidential Address to Lambeth called for a "Renewal of our Vocation as Bishops": ""we must never avoid the challenges of episcopal leadership. For that challenge is to follow our Lord in such simplicity of discipleship that our goodness, our holiness, our humility is there for all to see."[8] George Carey, in the courageous, costly and charitable role he played at Lambeth, fully lived up to this charge.

Another welcome innovation of Lambeth can be seen in the cooperation of First World evangelical Anglican leaders with African and Asian bishops in preparing and organizing Lambeth to preclude First World liberals from dominating the agenda. Position papers, friendly conference space, communications technology and media relations all contributed to a level playing field. The ugly charges by angry, frustrated liberal bishops that well-financed American conservative lobbies had bought the votes of African bishops, whose churches had only recently "moved out of animism into a very superstitious kind of Christianity,"[9] were embarrassingly incredible.

It was repeatedly emphasized, especially by liberal bishops, that Lambeth resolutions are neither legislative nor binding for Anglican

Churches. This is true, but not the whole truth. The theological and revisionist sexual agenda of liberal Anglicanism has been shown, dramatically, to be minoritarian, indeed sectarian, in the context of World Anglicanism, as well as Roman Catholic, Eastern Orthodox and most of Protestant and Pentecostal Christianity.

Lambeth and subsequent developments—notably the consecration by Bishops Tay (Singapore) and Kolini (Rwanda) of John Rogers, former Dean of Trinity Episcopal School for Ministry, and Charles Murphy, head of First Promise, as missionary bishops to America—have offered the hope of episcopal oversight for faithful Anglicans where territorial episcopacy has defaulted. Missionary bishops, trespassing on the territorial principle of Anglican episcopacy, present an alarming innovation, but a much worse case scenario in the eyes of many—including many Two-Thirds World bishops—would be to tolerate the censoring, exiling and excommunication of orthodox Anglicans. Pray God we will not see this happening in Canada.

Anglican Evangelical Theological Renaissance

Genuine renewal of Christian faith cannot be generated by scholarship alone, but deep and enduring renewal and reformation requires the loving and honouring of God with our minds as well as our hearts and souls. A great sign of hope in the latter part of the twentieth century has been the renaissance of scholarship that works creatively, critically and faithfully within the grand Christian meta-narrative. In vast areas of scholarly endeavour—research, production of books, articles, publishing of journals, conferencing, the establishment of new institutes, programs and seminaries, the revitalization of well-established schools and seminaries—evangelicals are in the midst of what can only be called a renaissance. In all of this, Anglican evangelicals have played a central role. One thinks of the quality of scholarship, education and training for ministry offered at such institutions as Wycliffe College, Toronto, Wycliffe Hall, Oxford, Trinity Episcopal School for Ministry, Ambridge, Pennsylvania and, not least, Regent College, Vancouver. Beyond teaching and scholarly production from within the most dynamic schools and seminaries, Anglican evangelicals have been awarded major theological chairs in world-class universities. Perhaps most important, evangelical writers, and Anglicans particularly, have served the crucially important readership for popular Christian literature, especially in apologetics and devotional writing. This corpus of fresh and faithful scholarship provides, as well, a rich store of resources for expository preaching and ministry of the Word. A walk through the Regent College Bookstore reminds one (somewhat dauntingly) that of the production and reading of good books there is no end.

Renewal in the Spirit: Alpha

Founded in 1980 in Holy Trinity, Brompton in London, England with Nicky Gumbel coming to leadership in 1990, the Alpha program reached critical mass and began to spread widely in 1993. Now, according to its website, more than 10,000 Alpha courses are running across 77 countries. Hundreds more register each month as church leaders from all denominations report the astonishing impact of the course on non-churchgoers and existing Christians in their areas. Presently it is spreading fast to many secular locations— prisons, businesses and schools—aimed especially at people who do not attend a church.

Many Anglicans are rightfully reserved when it comes to emotionally charged renewal ministries, adopting what might be called the Gamaliel principle (named after the Rabbi who taught Saint Paul): leave it alone; if it is of human origin it will self-destruct; if, however, it is from God, it will be unstoppable (Acts 5:34–39). Alpha has had such unstoppably positive results in Canadian Anglicanism that our Primate, Michael Peers, has given it the "Toronto Blessing"—what more could be asked? The spiritual awakening and empowerment authentically offered by Alpha, which has pioneered effective new means of presenting the Gospel of Christ in contemporary culture, is truly a powerful sign of hope.

The Gift of Liturgy

A final sign of hope can be discerned in the enduring appeal of classical Anglican worship—orderly, beautiful, scripturally infused, Christocentric, mindful of the saints who have gone before, surrounding us with a great cloud of witnesses and adorned with skilled musicianship and hymnody. If the Prayer Book cadences of Elizabethan English and Cranmerian rhetoric are not for everyone, the classic elements of the historical liturgy, faithfully updated, are a priceless gift to Christian worship—awaiting those, especially, who are parched spiritually by user-friendly, chorus-driven, "non-liturgical" liturgies. It is remarkable how many former free-church evangelicals, especially Brethren, end up in their maturity devoted to Anglican liturgy. Once you have tasted deeply, it is hard to go back.

CONCLUSION

What is the future of World Anglicanism? There are many themes, trends and issues that I have necessarily omitted: ecumenical and inter-faith relations, the ministry of women, issues of justice, church-state relations, to mention but a few lacunae. However, the themes that have been identified—trends of global religious demography, theology, leadership formation and spiritual renewal—all give good reason, I believe, for genuine hope. But in all candour, we cannot predict the future with any assurance of accuracy. History is a perpetual store of contingency and surprise. It is likely that First World Anglicanism will face increasing turbulence in the near future. I believe that episcopal leadership from Asia, Africa and Latin America will likely play a salutary role in helping to reaffirm the essential tenets of Anglican Christianity. Indeed, only by reaffirming this centre, this historical heart of Anglican faith, can we avoid the tragedy of schism.

It is this task—the reaffirmation of the centre in classic Anglican doctrine, discipline, liturgy and devotion—that inspires the mission of the Essentials partnership. It is our hope that the legacy of the

Essentials 2001 National Conference—with its theme "Lift High the Cross: Global Anglicanism and the Future of the Anglican Church of Canada"—will contribute positively to the life and unity of our Church as centred in Christ.

But let us remember that our hope is neither in the future, nor in the Anglican Church, *per se.* Our hope is in God; and, as Saint Paul assures, this "hope does not disappoint us, because God has poured out his love into our hearts by the Holy Spirit, whom he has given us."[10]

It is an exciting, if daunting, time to be testing a call to ordained Anglican ministry. Two things are assured: faithful leadership of high quality will be urgently needed, and those who respond to God's call will live in interesting times.

ENDNOTES

[1] George Egerton, ed., *Anglican Essentials: Reclaiming Faith Within the Anglican Church of Canada* (Toronto: Anglican Book Centre, 1995).

[2] Reginald Bibby, *Unknown Gods: the Ongoing Story of Religion in Canada* (Toronto: Stoddart, 1993), 1.

[3] Alan Wolfe, "The Pursuit of Autonomy," *New York Times Magazine,* Sunday, 7 May 2000, p. 53.

[4] "Report of the Diocesan Commission on Levels of Ministry to Diocesan Synod May 1989," *Convening Circular and Synod Journal,* Diocese of New Westminster, 1989.

[5] *Catechism of the Catholic Church* (San Francisco: Ignatius Press, U.S. English translation, 1994).

[6] *International Bulletin of Missionary Research* 24, no. 1 (April 2000): 49.

[7] James Rosenthal, ed., *The Essential Guide To The Anglican Communion* (Harrisburg, PA: Morehouse Pub., 1998), 5–26.

[8] *The Official Report of the Lambeth Conference 1998* (Harrisburg, PA : Morehouse Pub.,1999), 12.

[9] James Solheim, *Diversity or Disunity?: Reflections on Lambeth 1998* (New York: Church Pub.,1999), 45.

[10] Romans 5:5

CHAPTER 2

THE CENTRALITY OF HOLY SCRIPTURE IN ANGLICANISM

J. I. Packer

I begin by giving some attention to the question, "What is Anglicanism, anyway?" One could talk about actual Anglicanism and describe the Anglican communion institutionally as an international fellowship, with its provinces, dioceses and parochial structures, and one can continue on that level if that is what one wants to do, but that is not what I want to do. I want to think about and tune into ideal Anglicanism—the Anglicanism that ought to be, the Anglicanism against which we measure the Anglicanism that actually is. I feel in myself, still, in my seventies, the concern to think in these terms, which I began to feel—and to feel strongly—more than half a century ago.

I am a "cradle Anglican" who became a convictional Anglican. I was born and brought up Anglican, by inertia, as you might say, and then the Lord Jesus got hold of me, and I became an Anglican by necessity, because my judgment under God anchored me in Anglicanism as the best place, and so the right place, for me to be. However, I can tell you honestly, all through those years of being a convictional Anglican, being an Anglican has been thoroughly uncomfortable, because actual Anglicanism has been so far from ideal Anglicanism. So, stay with me while I pursue this line of thought.

THE FRAMEWORK: IDEAL ANGLICANISM

What is ideal Anglicanism? What is authentic Anglicanism—by which I mean that when you see it, you say, "That's the real thing"? Well, I will explore seven major items—what I think are *the* seven major items by which anyone would identify Anglicanism, whatever particular group within Anglicanism they might link up with, and I am sure they are not strange to you.

A Catholic Goal

First, ideal Anglicanism has a *catholic goal*—that is, it aims to be a form of Christianity that neither adds to Christ's Christianity nor subtract from it; it seeks, rather, to embrace the whole of Christ's Christianity, maintaining all of it and teaching all of it. It wants, in other words, to be Christianity without distortion or diminution, and it is always checking to make sure that nothing that belongs to Christ's Christianity has got lost, just as it is always checking that nothing has crept in that doesn't belong to Christ's Christianity and ought not, therefore, to be there.

Biblical Foundations

With this catholic goal, secondly, ideal Anglicanism has *biblical foundations*. Now we come straight away to what it is that I am going to address here. Let us be clear that to have biblical foundations is one of the elements in Christ's Christianity: the principle that Scripture has authority goes back to the teaching of the Saviour and the apostles. One of the unhappy things about the past half-century in which I've been trying to make that point in public is that so very few people in the church seem to see it. The Anglican way is to acknowledge the sufficiency (meaning, both the adequacy and the authority) of Holy Scripture: a compendium of sixty-six books, which Article 6 of the thirty-nine declares were never matters of doubt in the church—that is, of corporate doubt in the church—at any time. (What the Article denies is not individual uncertainty about particular books—as we know, and as our Reformers knew, there was some of that—but corporate uncertainty. By the guidance of the Holy Spirit, there never was corporate uncertainty about any of these sixty-six books that constitute the canon today.) To acknowledge their canonicity— that is, to acknowledge their place as a rule and standard of faith and life—is fundamental to Christ's Christianity. It is, in other words, a catholic position, and something very basic, on which, as you know, our Reformation formularies are very strong. They needed to be in the sixteenth century, and they were made so. Therefore you have Article 20 referring explicitly to Holy Scripture as God's word written and going on to say, in effect, that in interpreting it, we are to understand that it is internally consistent. After all, how could God contradict himself? The Article reads as follows: "As it is not lawful for the Church to ordain anything that is contrary to God's word written, neither may it so expound one place of Scripture that it be repugnant to another." You do not need me to tell you that the violation of this Article is one of the besetting sins of theological leaders today both in the Anglican Church and in other churches. Here is our Article, then, testifying over nearly 500 years that this is not the right way to go. We are to acknowledge the internal consistency and coherence of all biblical teaching, and we are to have a conscience about making sure that we do not drift from any part of it. It comes from God; it is truth and wisdom from God. It is—and should be acknowledged as—sufficient for salvation. In the providence of God, everything we need to know for life and godliness is in Scripture, and Article 6 says this.

In a broader sense, the Anglican testimony ever since the Reformation has been to insist that support for one's soul and guidance for one's life is there in Scripture, and that every Christian must learn to draw that wisdom and support from Scripture. To that end, as you know, our Reformers devised a lectionary, which, if followed on a daily basis, would take all Anglican worshipers through the Old Testament once and the New Testament twice (and much of it three times) in any calendar year, in addition to taking us through the Psalter once a month. The Anglican vision at the time of the Reformation was that the Lord's people should soak themselves in Scripture as the means to their spiritual health. I will not dilate on how far we have got from that; just saying what I have said surely communicates that message. If this is ideal Anglicanism, it was also in actual fact the Anglicanism that existed in the sixteenth century, until things began to happen that changed the Anglican way. I think at this point you'll have to agree that with regard to Holy Scripture purifying, edifying and constantly revitalizing the church, as was the Reformers' goal, we have lost over the centuries rather more than we have gained.

A Reformational Heritage

A third quality in ideal Anglicanism is that it has a *Reformational heritage*. This great emphasis on the Bible is, of course, itself part of the Reformational heritage, but there is more to it than that. In the sixteenth century, the Church of England (the Anglican church, *Ecclesia Anglicana*) *washed its face*—that is what we should be saying. The testimony to the face washing process is in the Thirty-Nine Articles from which I quoted earlier, plus the basic *Book of Common Prayer*—Cranmer's 1552 book, which became England's 1662 book, which is the heart of Canada's 1962 book. There is also a third source of material that came out of the face washing process, and that is the *Book of Homilies*. That book is difficult to get hold of these days, and probably very few of us have ever read the *Homilies*. I'm going to quote from a bit of one of the Homilies later, but here I will just refer to the fact that the *Book of Homilies* exists and note that it is a vivid testimony to the adjusted, reformed, spruced-up Christianity that our Reformers had in view. In language, style and culture the sermons contained in the *Book of Homilies* show their age and may seem merely quaint, but at the level of principle they delineate the Reformational understanding of godliness with landmark authority, and if we do not know them it is our loss.

The sprucing up, the face washing, the adjusting and the correcting had to come, on the one hand, in the area of salvation: sovereign grace, original sin, justification by faith and the power of faith, which brings repentance out of the heart and transforms the life. On the other hand, the church needed to be reconceived primarily as a fellowship of believers out of whose common life comes the functioning of clergy, who within a preaching and teaching frame administer the two sacraments that Christ instituted—rather than as primarily a given structure of apostolically ordained priests and sacraments to which lay people adhere for salvation. This was a reversing, in fact, of the way in which then, and still, the Roman Catholic Church has seen itself. For Anglicans, the fellowship comes first. Our ecclesiology begins there. This Reformational heritage runs through our foundation documents and is to be included in our definition of ideal Anglicanism, because it is scriptural at every point.

A Liturgical Heritage

Fourth, we have a *liturgical heritage*, superb in quality, which reflects the common-sense awareness that when together as we address our God and Saviour—God who made and sustains the heavens and the earth, the great God of the Bible—we should do as we do when we sing hymns—that is, we should agree in advance on the words that we are going to use in order to speak to God more reverently, pointedly, unanimously and economically.

This is the liturgical rule for corporate worship. There was never any dispute in the church about its propriety; the church was producing liturgies from its earliest days. Of course it is also true—and those of us who are evangelicals know this very well—that one of the gifts of salvation is the gift of adoption, and since we are children in the Father's family, there would be something lacking if we did not call out spontaneously from our hearts to our heavenly Father, just the way that children call out what is in their minds and hearts to their earthly parents. If you didn't feel you could be free in talking to your heavenly Father, something would be wrong. Therefore the Anglican way has always been to encourage full freedom of that kind in private prayer, alongside our liturgical structure for common worship.

It is an unhappy thing, I think, that in more recent times, merely because of 1662 and its aftermath, our Free Church brothers and sisters in the gospel have been so suspicious of set forms for public worship and made so many Anglicans feel uneasy about them. Liturgy is common sense, and in the form in which we have inherited it, it is biblical common sense. The Prayer Book liturgy has been described as simply the Bible arranged for worship. So indeed it is; there is hardly a phrase anywhere in the Prayer Book that has not in one way or another got a biblical precedent. Our liturgy is the responsive, worshiping echo of what God tells us in his Word.

Have you ever noticed that Archbishop Cranmer, in putting together all his main services, displayed marvelous wisdom in employing a blindingly simple device that gives them more evangelical power than the users of them have ever been able to put into words? That power has been felt in countless Anglican congregations who, generation after generation, have grown in grace and in the knowledge of Christ through the Prayer Book, in a way for which one can never be too thankful or praise God too much. What was the device? Simply this: to build the services out of the sequence of *sin* detected, then *grace* proclaimed, and finally *faith* expressed in multiple ways, whereby sinners lay hold of the grace that has just been declared, give thanks for it and recommit themselves to live by it. Used three times with ascending intensity, it gives our classic Eucharistic liturgy enormous power. The sequence is first set out in general terms in the Ante-Communion; then it is expressed more poignantly in the discomfort of personal confession of sin, followed by the comfort of the prayer of absolution and the assurances of grace from God, for which the *Sursum Corda* is faith voicing gratitude; and then its third appearance is its sacramental embodiment in the canon—the communion—the consecration of ourselves, which theologically is a single flow of prayerful devotion, rounded off by the rhapsodic *Gloria*. Latter-day revisers have disrupted this structure to no good effect that I can see; here, at any rate, the old is most certainly better. It is the use of this sequence that also gives Morning and Evening Prayer such a fundamental feeling of rightness as we first confess our sins, then hear the grace of pardon for sin declared, and then move into prayer and praise as we lay hold of that grace afresh. Then comes the reading of God's Word, and as grateful, forgiven sinners, we listen and we learn. Richard Hooker was absolutely right when he said that the reading of the lessons in public worship is God preaching to instruct us, and the lessons ought to be read in a way that shows that the reader understands that. And the rest of what we do—gratefully confessing together the faith that God has given us, interceding out of love for others who need our prayers and seeking to profit from the sermon— all comes out of the joy, assurance and gratitude for the forgiveness of our sins with which the service started.

There it is! We cannot wonder that discerning folk outside the Anglican communion often reveal, as I do not know how many have revealed to me, "Oh yes, we use the Prayer Book in our private devotions, even if not in our public ministry." Thank God for Cranmer and his wisdom in putting the Prayer Book together so wonderfully. This, then, is the fourth element—the liturgical heritage of Prayer Book worship that is integral to Anglicanism.

A Pastoral and Evangelistic Ethos

Fifth, ideal Anglicanism has a characteristic *pastoral and evangelistic ethos*. Alas, this ethos has not always been exhibited in congregations— that is the story now and has been the story down through the centuries—but it is very clear in the Prayer Book that this is how it is meant to be. Do not ever allow it to be said that until George Whitefield and John Wesley began their work in the eighteenth century the Church of England knew nothing about evangelism. I know that Whitefield and Wesley are almost cult heroes, and so they should be; I know that when we think of evangelism today we think of the sort of outreach in which they constantly engaged, and about which they were very up front and explicit—but the Church of England has, in fact, been doing evangelism ever since the Reformation. That is what the catechism, the confirmation service and the so-little-used exhortations in the Holy Communion service are all about. It is institutional evangelism rather than itinerant or "big tent" evangelism. It is ongoing evangelism, week by week, rather than what I hope you'll forgive me for calling "spasm" evangelism, in which there are a few days of very intense evangelistic effort and then a slacking off.

This is made as plain as can be in the bishop's admonition in the Ordinal to the priests being ordained. I was once on a commission in Britain where an attempt was being made to draft a new Ordinal, and some on the commission wanted to cut out this long, admonitory sermon that the Bishop is charged to read, but finally the attempt was given up because, as someone said with resignation, "The bishops love reading this admonition and do not want to stop." Well, good for the bishops! It should be read—it is vital, central and magnificent. Any who are thinking of Anglican ordination need to hear well this section of the admonition before proceeding any further:

> We exhort you, in the name of our Lord Jesus Christ, that you have in remembrance, into how high a dignity, and to how weighty an office and charge you are called, that is to say, to be messengers, watchmen, and stewards of the Lord, to teach and to premonish [an old word for admonish], to feed and provide for the Lord's family; to seek for Christ's sheep that are dispersed abroad, and for his children who are in the midst of this sinful world, that they may be saved through Christ for ever.

"To seek for Christ's sheep that are dispersed abroad"—that is evangelism. The expectation in the sixteenth century, reflecting the social order of things in those days, was that families would be the units of the church. The minister, catechizing the children after the second lesson in Evening Prayer each Sunday, would be pursuing all that needs to be pursued evangelistically when one is evangelizing young people. In the presence of their parents, who would be sitting in the congregation, the children would be taught from the catechism, and they would be nourished in the faith at home as well, and in due course come to confirmation, where they would be making before the church a personal profession of faith, thus qualifying themselves for admission to the Lord's table. That is evangelism —institutional family evangelism— and whatever else is happening in our own congregations today, such evangelism ought to be going on there in some shape or form. The weakening of the family as a spiritual unit, and the placing of Sunday Schools during service time (when I was a boy, Sunday Schools met in the afternoon) has changed the sociology, but the priority of evangelizing and nurturing the rising generation remains. We need to check over what we do in our Sunday Schools to make sure that this actually is happening.

I have been concerned about evangelistic and pastoral ministry all through my life as a teacher, to the point that I have never really felt comfortable when I have not had some small share in the ongoing work of a parish congregation. The academic work that I do appears to me as my way of extending what I do when I am given opportunity to preach and teach in church. It is ministry to the Lord's people as the Ordinal defines it, and in my case, particularly to those special people who are going to be tomorrow's clergy. So I am concerned that everything that I teach in college, as in the pulpit, should have a practical application and that those I teach should see clearly what it is. No one who teaches in a seminary or seminary-type institution ought, I think, to feel any different from that. I, for one, feel this deeply, and so I say it with some emphasis.

A Rational Temper

Sixth, Anglicanism is also characterized by a *rational temper*. In Anglicanism you can raise any question, and the Anglican way is to pursue the question, with full respect for the questioner, through the discipline of debate. There have been church communities in

Christendom where the way of dealing with folk who come up with unorthodox ideas is to use the "big stick," disciplining them immediately by exclusion: "You can't continue with us unless you give up these ideas." The Anglican way has always been to talk it out. This has made for untidiness in the Anglican Church at just about every period of its life, but what it shows us first of all is—if I understand the Anglican ethos rightly at this point—respect for the image of God in each other. God made us rational, and that means that when we have problems and puzzles, we ought to talk them out. That procedure expresses, secondly, confidence in the discipline of debate, and the value of thrashing things through in discussion, so that one is able to say, "Now everything's on the table, just look and you'll see what the truth is!" At least you *should* see what the truth is. Anglicans know—though they have never made a big deal of it—that sometimes what our Catholic brothers call "invincible ignorance" takes over, and people confronted with compelling arguments against their position still do not see it. As Luther once said, "They resist even though they cannot resist." But that is just the unhappy fallout in individual cases of a process that, in itself, is thoroughly salutary. It does call for patience, and the Anglican way is to be patient. We are battling our way at the moment through debates on homosexuality just as for two generations and more we have battled our way through all kinds of discussions about bringing the faith up to date. We do not use the big stick; in faith and hope we go on discussing—until God, in His mercy, through the discussions, brings us to a common mind. That, as I said, is part of the Anglican way. You see, then, why I always wince a bit when I meet—as I do meet—Anglican brothers and sisters who say, "I am losing patience with the Anglican church, I see how disorderly it is, I look into the future, I think the disorder is going to continue, I'm going to leave." I do not believe that is ordinarily the way or will of God, and I do not believe that those who lose patience and leave finally profit as a result of what they have done. So when, in our own congregations, people come up with strange ideas, by the grace of the Holy Spirit we should practice patience and debate the matter with them on a one-to-one basis. That is Anglican ministry, or one very important dimension of it. Nobody gets "dumbed down" in proper Anglican ministry; no one is made to feel stupid; no one is made to feel, "Well, you mustn't ask that question, you mustn't explore that view. Now shut your eyes and swallow the orthodoxy that I'm just about to force down your throat." We do not resolve matters that way, and I think this is one of the strengths of Anglicanism in the long run.

Episcopal Leadership

The final thing the Anglican Church is committed to is *episcopal leadership* as one form of the larger reality of clergy leadership. In the past, Anglicanism's historic episcopate has rightly been valued for maintaining visible churchly continuity and caring for parish clergy; here, however, it is the role of the bishop as leader that I want to stress. What Anglicans of earlier generations felt in their bones was that every presbyter is a local-church bishop, just as every diocesan bishop is a presbyter—not in terms of the details of a job description (bishops have extra tasks that are all their own), but in terms of how they stand in their pastoral relation to the people put under their care. Clergy as such are to safeguard, yes, and they are also to lead. To settle for simply keeping the wheels turning round—whether in the congregation or in the diocese—is not enough, and deep down we all know that that is not enough. There is an element of prophetic vision, pastoral initiative and soul-winning outreach that we who are clergy—and most certainly those of us who are bishops—are called to cultivate. God is always calling the church to reach out and move forward in ministry, and in this it is our responsibility to lead; that is the Anglican view of the ordained ministry as such. In the case of diocesan bishops, the obligation is there in double strength, so to speak. This is the essential Anglican way to celebrate diocesan episcopacy as enhancing the well-being of the church, and I support it, as surely we all do. As we think of this, however, we do well to remember that at a bishop's consecration the following dialogue takes place between the Archbishop and himself:

The Archbishop: Will you…faithfully exercise yourself in the…holy Scriptures, and call upon God by prayer, for the true understanding of the same; so as ye may be able by them to teach and exhort with wholesome doctrine, and to withstand and convince the gainsayers?

Answer: I will do so, by the help of God.

The Archbishop: Are you ready, with all faithful diligence, to banish and drive away all erroneous and strange doctrine contrary to God's Word; and both privately and openly to call upon and encourage others to do the same?

Answer: I am ready, the Lord being my helper.

THREE QUESTIONS

Now I will raise three questions about the things I have said. First, by what right do I speak of this profile of ideal Anglicanism as the authentic Anglicanism, Anglicanism as it always ought to be? The answer is, by right of the constitution and by right of history. I think that there can be no doubt that my profile of ideal Anglicanism is loyal to the constitution, and you will remember the Solemn Declaration of 1893 that committed the Anglican Church of Canada to stay with historical Anglicanism at all points. Until the nineteenth century all Anglicanism was committed to the principles I have described, and Anglican life and ministry proceeded in this way. In the nineteenth and twentieth centuries mainstream Anglicanism continued on this path, although these centuries saw more in the way of what I am going to call "revisionist eccentricities" than had been seen in earlier days.

I hope it is clear that I am not "talking party" when I speak positively of these things. I have not used that word, and I am not thinking in the party way. Yes, I was indeed nurtured as an evangelical in the days when, in both the Church of England and the Anglican Church of Canada, evangelicalism was regarded as a party position—as it still is, by those who do not agree with it. But what I am trying to speak of now is mainstream Anglicanism as distinct from "eccentric" Anglicanism. Eccentric Anglicanism means simply "out of the centre."

Each of the nineteenth-century parties in the Church of England, which were duly exported to Canada, Australia and other parts of the Anglican world, had important goals but lacked mainstream breadth. The evangelicals were after Reformational theology and powerful evangelistic ministry. The so-called "Catholic-revival" people were after patristic theology and the recovery of "churchliness" at a deep level. Those called "broad-churchmen"—the grandfathers of modern liberals and radicals— wanted effective communication, Christianity expressed in a way that those shaped by the changing culture could grasp and see to be relevant to ongoing community life. Several things went wrong: evangelicals thought that the Catholic stream in the church was a conspiracy to try and take Anglicans back to Rome; the Anglo-Catholics thought that the evangelical understanding of assurance and joy in Christ was sheer sentimentality and contemptible for that reason; and the broad-churchmen were betrayed into believing that the world always has the wisdom and the church must always be playing catch-up, even at the cost of watering down its inherited beliefs, lowering its standards of faithful discipleship and replacing its proven style of liturgy with something flashier. The belief that such changes will make it easier to communicate the faith, when the changes themselves diminish the faith, is one of the great fallacies of the last hundred years, and it is a sad thing that anybody should still be embracing it. But I must not pursue that thought at present.

Second, what is the value of this historic Anglican heritage? This may be the real question for many who are wondering if they should seek entry into Anglican ministry rather than ministry somewhere else in the Christian world. My answer to this question is that the

Anglican heritage—for nurture, the formation of believers and the glorifying of God through worship—is the wisest and richest that the world has ever seen. That is not, in my estimate, an overstatement, and I think I know enough about Christian history to make the assertion responsibly. It is the richness and, as I think, the right-mindedness of the heritage that keeps me an Anglican today.

Third, what is the future of this heritage? My answer is that it depends on whether God visits us with repentance and renewed blessing, and that remains to be seen. What we have to do is to work and pray and see what the God of surprises will do for us in the Anglican church of the twenty-first century.

In saying all of the above, I have established my framework for the rest of what I have to say about the centrality of Scripture in Anglicanism. To rehabilitate that centrality—which, as I have shown, is fundamental to the vision of Anglicanism as it should be—is now my direct goal, and all that follows is spoken to that end.

THE CENTRALITY OF HOLY SCRIPTURE IN IDEAL ANGLICANISM

What is the Bible? In this day and age, I think we are in a better position than any previous Christian generation to give the proper answer to that question. Modern study has displayed most fully the extraordinary range of material and variety of presentation—from the human standpoint, that is—in the sixty-six books that make up our canonical Bible. There is history, which is the backbone of the Bible story—from Genesis right through to the Gospels and the Book of Acts—all recounted with great literary skill so as to communicate theology by its arrangement and style. There are sermons and theological declarations explaining the significance of this history as it relates to God's chosen people—the Old Testament prophets do this in their messages, and the New Testament apostles do it in their letters, which are simply sermons on paper. There are hymns and prayers and meditations of all kinds in the Psalter. There are philosophical reflections and counsels for the covenanted in the wisdom books of the Old Testament and in the book of James in the New Testament. There is a love lyric, the Song of Solomon, which is surely an extended parable of the love of God for his people and the proper way in which the Lord's people should respond to his love. And there are the fantastic apocalyptic visions of Daniel and Revelation, which tell us that God is leading history to a triumphant conclusion, which his battered people will share and enjoy. Such is the Bible: a wonder both for its outward variety as for its inner unity. Do we ourselves value it at its true worth?

We stand, as I said, at the end of two centuries of work that have highlighted the richness of the humanity of the Bible and the variety of its contents as they have never been highlighted before. If now we link that appreciation of the Bible's humanness with a Reformational appreciation of its God-givenness, we shall have the concept of Holy Scripture that we need. It is one hundred percent human, and it is one hundred percent divine. The recognition that this is so is what has been lost. Up until the nineteenth century, Christendom was agreed on the canon, the inspiration and, in broad terms, the authoritative status of this Holy Scripture. The disagreements were only about interpretation—who should do it and what the place of tradition and the organized church should be in the process. There was vigorous debate over these matters in the sixteenth century, because the disagreements were real. In the nineteenth and the twentieth centuries, however, solvents were applied to the biblical faith of the Protestant churches in a way that was calculated to dissolve that faith so that it would quite simply cease to be. At the academic level, at any rate, this is largely what happened.

One solvent, which emerged in the early nineteenth century and had various sources, was skepticism—both about the Christian facts as Scripture records them and about biblical revelation itself. Those who followed the philosopher Kant and the theologian Schleiermacher turned their backs on the idea that what is written in the canon is revelation from God. They did not have the wit to see that they were turning their backs on the truth that God, who made us in his image and gave us the gift of language, is capable himself of using language to tell us things—and has in fact done so in the ministry of his own incarnate Son, as well as in the canonical writings. That is the blockage that skepticism about biblical revelation led to, however.

Another solvent was rationalism—the attitude of arrogance that emerged with the so-called Enlightenment—which claims that man is the measure of all things and that the human mind can solve all problems. Rationalism set itself to cut Christianity down to intelligible size. Doctrines that have transcendence and mystery built into them, such as the Trinity, and the full truth of the Incarnation and the Atonement, were simply jettisoned by the rationalistic reconstructors of Christianity. And biblical criticism—the child of skepticism and rationalism—began to assert that nobody with any sense would trust the Bible in its record of facts. Evolutionism also came in as an alternative ideology to the biblical understanding that God created the world, that it was good, that it went bad through human folly and that God is now in the process of redeeming, restoring and remaking it. The evolutionary idea is that everything, including religion, started pretty primitive and rough, but is getting better as time goes on. Because of it, *progress* became the great nineteenth century ideology; belief in the certainty of progress was both the fruit and the expression of the evolutionary mentality, a mentality stemming not just from Darwin, but from German philosophers who were talking evolution from the beginning of the nineteenth century. I do not think we have to bother very much about that mentality nowadays; evolutionary optimism reversed itself in the twentieth century as the world lapsed back into barbarism and the infliction of human agony and distress in just about every imaginable way.

But a further factor operates today, which is postmodernism—the disillusioned denial of the rationalism of the Enlightenment, which in these days we call the rationalism of modernity. Postmodernism is a counsel of despair: it tells us that there is no public truth, no public wisdom, no public "rightness" or "wrongness"—you just do as you think and never mind the rest of the human community. "My truth

is my truth, your truth is your truth, and never the twain shall meet."
I do not think postmodernism can last, but it is riding high at the
moment and I'm sure that it has another twenty years of life in it,
though probably not more.

Since these factors have come into our situation, unbelief of the
Bible is now at a premium. In the pews, people are simply bewildered;
all they are sure of is that the clergy tell them that you cannot trust
the Bible any more, and the clergy are modeling this lack of trust in
their ministries. In the seminaries, alas, there is a habit of encouraging
the way-out, enterprising thinkers who follow this track of leaving
the Bible behind and developing their own theologies in the way
that learned people have been doing all through the nineteenth and
twentieth centuries—that is, seeing what ideas the reading of the
Bible and the study of the church's tradition trigger in one's own
imagination and pursuing them. Persons who get sent to theological
teaching institutions where this is happening have their minds stuffed
with this kind of theologizing and then, just like schoolmasters, they
go out and teach what they were taught, and perhaps go on doing so
for the next forty years. Some parishes are suffering simply because of
the way their clergy were educated. This shouts aloud to high heaven
for the adjustments that need to be made to get us back on track,
with the Bible once again taking the place that, in Anglicanism, it is
meant to have.

What is our task for tomorrow, then, in relation to the Bible?
Four things, I suggest. First, teach! It has been said that for the
ordained ministry: "Priority one is to teach, priority two is to teach,
and priority three is to teach." We clergy should have a conscience
whereby we ask ourselves at the end of each day, "What teaching
have I done today? To whom have I taught what?" We have got to
teach the Bible; therefore we must ourselves be masters of the biblical
text, soaking ourselves in Scripture as our reformers directed that we
should. Bishop Stephen Neill once said that if the vision of Cranmer's
lectionary had been fulfilled, the Church of England would be the
greatest Bible-reading church in Christendom today. I apply that and

say, we who are in ministry in the Anglican Church of Canada most certainly ought to be the greatest Bible readers in Christendom today, marinated in the Scriptures so that we are able to teach the Scriptures. One of the problems facing theological institutions all across Canada is that every generation of students now comes in knowing less about the Bible than did the generation before. There is a lot of lost ground to be made up every time this happens. There are today a lot of folk in the ordained ministry who do not know their Bibles well, because they got an education that did not require them to do so.

Task number two goes with task number one: encourage Bible reading as a discipline for every Anglican. This is an age in which the culture, at a popular level anyway, is discouraging any reading except for purely technical purposes. The assumption is that it is much better to see everything dramatized—to watch the television or go to see a movie—than to settle down to read books—serious books, and sometimes long books—in the way that our ancestors did. We have to tackle that head on, I think, in the people to whom we minister and tell them—or *show* them—how much they are missing by not reading or by not thinking about what they read (as one would never be found thinking about the things that one sees on television). One of the truths about multi-media presentations is that the more senses you engage in what Marshall McLuhan called "cool communication" (with television, of course, it is both sight and hearing), the less thinking you will do. In fact the multi-media impact shapes you into a sponge, whose mental energy is used in simply sucking up what is set before you. I root for reading, "hot communication" in McLuhan's words, in which you must exercise your mind on the text. We have to encourage people every way we can to read the Bible—to read it as individuals and to read it at home with their families.

The third thing we must do is maintain the authority of the Bible as the Bible interprets itself; that is to say, we must maintain the authority of the apostolic teaching. The apostles' report in the New Testament of God's teaching through Christ, and their own witness to God's saving work through him, must be maintained as the resource that throws the light on—and so enables you to interpret—everything in the Old Testament. That is the Christian way to read the Old Testament; the Lord and the apostles were already doing it, and we are to follow in their footsteps. When we are confronted with those who want to part company with the Lord and with the apostles at this point, we must challenge them in the name of the authority of Scripture.

The fourth and final thing is that we clergy and would-be clergy must become models of living by biblical truth and maintaining biblical standards at every point. Those who swim against the current stream by contending for biblical authority are going to be looked at very critically; our personal lives are going to be watched. When Jesus said, "Let your light so shine before men that they may see your good works and glorify your Father in heaven," he was plainly talking about good works backing up good words. He was not saying, as they used to say in England in my youth, "Samaritanship is just as good as verbal witness." Not so—Jesus is calling for both the one and the other. He is assuming the verbal witness and adding, "Let your lives give credibility to the things you say, because failures in living will undermine the credibility of your spoken word." Credibility will either be added or credibility will be reduced by our behaviour. God help us!

Here, then, is the fourfold challenge to us as we think of the centrality of Holy Scripture in the ideal Anglicanism that we are seeking, by God's grace, to make real in the actual Anglicanism of the twenty-first century. It is a challenge we dare not evade. I say again, God help us.

CHAPTER 3

THE FUTURE OF
ORDAINED MINISTRY

George Sumner

I was ordained in Dudoma, Tanzania. My own bishop in the United States came over to ordain me, and he was very ambitious—he wanted to ordain me in Swahili. The translator gave him a little piece of paper with the ordination service translated into Swahili, the words written out syllable by syllable, so that he would know how to pronounce them. He's a wonderful man, but he's a little forgetful, and he had left his reading glasses in the Diocesan office. I was sitting there in the front row of the Cathedral, and I knew I was in trouble when I saw him holding the pamphlet really close to his face, then further away. Finally I came forward, and he found my head. The Swahili word for priest is *kasisi,* and the word for church is *kamisa.* He put his hands on my head, and he couldn't quite see the paper, so he said, "George, I ordain you as a *church* within Christ's church!" Now, most Anglican clergy think they are laws unto themselves—and I really am! But that will not be true for you; you will be ordained as *priests* within the worldwide church.

Fifteen years ago I traveled to the southwest of the United States for an interview, to see if I should be the vicar of an Anglican mission on a Navajo reservation. After one day in Fort Defiance, I felt that my decision had been made for me. The interim rector, an alcoholic, sat in the dark, putting down tumbler after tumbler of scotch, as he slurred the sad story of that place on into the evening. One of the previous vicars had been a sexual abuser. There was no Sunday school, no youth group, no Bible study, but there was plenty of inter-clan fighting, plenty of broken-down buildings inhabited by feral cats and plenty of red ink. When Bishop Frenzdorf of Navajo arrived the next day, I told him in no uncertain terms, "Thanks, but no thanks. This place is sick," to which he replied, "You're right. Everything you've heard is true, and let me tell you a couple of scandals you may have missed." He proceeded to do so in lurid detail. The bishop denied nothing; he varnished nothing; and when we started our three-hour trip over the mountain back to the Diocesan office, I assumed that I was heading toward the end of this sorry venture. Yet as the miles went by, slowly and by degrees, like a skilled captain turning a boat, he began to talk about Good Shepherd Mission as a challenge. He wondered aloud how someone under priestly vows could turn his or her back on such a poor, wandering place. And by the top of that mountain, an hour into the trip, I was wondering what duty required. When the pickup rolled into Farmington, New Mexico, I'll be darned if I wasn't actually excited about the possibilities of the place.

What is the lesson of this—other than to be wary of clever bishops? I hope I will be able to take you over the same mountain. You see, the harsh things you think about the church are all true. And let me tell you a few more, in case you missed one: it is biblically illiterate; it is culturally and morally compromised; it is a church that cannot tell the doctrine of the atonement from a lamp stand. It is shrinking, squabbling, maybe broke—and yet, in spite of all that, incredibly proud. By God's grace I hope that you will see, when the pickup rolls in, what a wonderful time this is to serve God as an ordained minister of the good news of Jesus Christ in the Anglican Church.

So, what is the future of the ordained ministry? That is a doubly difficult question, since we are so unclear about it in the present! The role has lost its sheen of cultural prestige. Our churches ache, and yet our clergy seem ill-equipped as evangelists. That same bishop, Wesley Frenzdorf of Navajoland, was part of a movement reaching back to the theology of the missionary Roland Allen, who was in China in the early 1900s. It is a movement that is dominant in a number of dioceses throughout North America and in the Anglican Church of Canada, and it rightly emphasizes the ministry of the whole people of God, often called "total ministry." Amidst so much that is right about that movement, it can sometimes sound as if the ordained clergy are the central problem, and that their future is mainly a matter of getting out of the way! One might put our task this way: how can we keep all that is good about the baptismal revolution, the revolution of total ministry, and at the same time have a positive vision of the unique vocation of the ordained? But the truth is that the problem cuts deeper. Holy orders are for the ordering of the church. In other words, our job, by God's grace, is to see that the church is ordered to the right end, to see that it is pointed towards the right goal. So, confusion about ordained ministry is what the doctors and therapists call a "presenting symptom," but the *disease* is confusion about the purpose of the church itself. Therefore, "amen" and "hurrah" for confusion about the ordained ministry—*if*, and only if, it raises the important question of what the church is for. Of course, the place to turn to answer fundamental questions like that one is the Word of God. I will enlist the help of St. Paul twice—first to answer the question about the nature of the church itself, and then to understand the place of the pastor (or priest or presbyter) within that church. Let us turn first to St. Paul in 2 Corinthians:

> What we preach is not ourselves, but Jesus Christ as Lord, and ourselves as your servants for Jesus' sake. For it is the God who said, "Let light shine out of darkness," who shone in our hearts to give the light of the knowledge of the glory of God in the face of Christ. But we have this treasure in earthen vessels, to

show that transcendent power belongs to God, and not to us. (2 Cor 4:5–7)

"We have this treasure in earthen vessels." That is, I contend, the key passage that will enable Christians of our time to grasp the nature of the church. Note first that it is invariably a *treasure in a clay pot*—the two have to be distinguished, but never separated, and therein lies the rub. For it is easy, especially in our time, to imagine a disposable pot which is mere packaging for the gospel. On the other hand it is easy to merge the two in your mind. The evangelical error historically has been the first, to suppose that the church has a disposable function; the Catholic error has been the latter, to suppose that the clay is gold. On the contemporary scene, we may be tempted to come to theological college knowing that we have a ministry, and then looking for a church in which to exercise it—but that would suppose that the gospel could stand alone, apart from the clay works. However, on the very same scene, we might suppose that the church's job is to put a finger to the air, as if every doctrinal wind were the Holy Spirit—and there it is all dirt and no jewel. No, there is treasure in the pot, but it always comes within the earthenware. That is God's will, so that the glory will be his and not ours, we hear from St. Paul. That is God's will, so that the humility of the church can itself become an example of the lowliness with which the incarnate Lord came to us. It is God's will that the jewel should be in this clay pot, for he wants his grace to sink deeply into our bodies as well as our souls, but in such a way that we never mistake the head—the Lord—for the body.

Think with me for a moment about your home parish. Imagine a couple new to the parish, and indeed new to the Christian faith. They throw themselves in with both feet and, to be sure, the parish has no lack of committees and programs to put them in. After a year in they may not be burned out, but they are grilled at least medium-well done! There are more fights and foibles than they supposed, and most of it is also humdrum and unspiritual, and they begin to fade away. Maybe you were once part of that couple. Surely, as the newly ordained person, you will have to counsel them. At the very

51

heart of their story is the question of what "spiritual" means, and that goes back to Paul's metaphor. What is spirituality? It is simply focusing on the gospel, but right where the Lord promised it would be, inevitably in a broken clay pot. Discernment, humility, patience, zeal, forgiveness and hope—all of those are required equipment for every faithful parish Christian in the deceivingly simple task of distinguishing, but never separating, the treasure and the pot. The church, then, is by its very nature in an awkward state—chosen vessel of what it is not: the gospel treasure, the word about Christ and his indwelling Spirit. What if the ordained woman or man is simply the one whose life is dedicated to reminding the community of Christians that their blessing is in this awkward mode—the treasure and the pot—so simple, so mysterious. What would that mean? That would mean reminding our congregations, when they get lost in the Strawberry Festival or the Ailing Roof, that they are there for the gospel so that it does not get lost inside the leaking pot. And that would mean, particularly for evangelicals in our time, reminding Christians who are discouraged by the messiness and the sinfulness of the church that it is into this broken sinful vessel that Christ has poured his good news.

It will require enormous discernment and theological discrimination to figure out which way our parishes are listing, which message they need to hear. The task is unending, demanding this recurring act of wisdom. And it will require that we love them—the ones who are in our care—and pray ceaselessly for them and live sacrificially toward them, especially when they frustrate us, for that is the only way that they will be ready to hear when we point away from ourselves (and from them) and toward Jesus Christ. It means that we must identify deeply with them and yet maintain the distance that makes it possible to do the one thing needful. Needless to say, all of that is a tall order. We will get it wrong constantly, since we ourselves are nothing but clay pots containing the good news. The wonder is that by depending utterly on grace we will accomplish our task of pointing to Christ in and above his gathered people. We will do that as much in our failure as in our success.

There has been a great debate in the church through the centuries. The Catholics have tended to say that the priesthood has to do with who we are. The technical term is character—literally, "a stamp on the soul." And the Protestants have emphasized function—important tasks, assigned on behalf of the whole people of God, a whole priestly nation. But if we look at things in the way I am suggesting, then we can see the truth in what both have to say. To be sure, the ordained ministry is a function, a task: to point away from the congregation and ourselves toward Christ (often in the midst of a tsunami of activity that can carry any parish away). Ultimately the task is to force people to look at how God's grace is given—concretely, not abstractly—in their actual community. But the priest can only do this with his or her whole life. The priest can only be that kind of sign if the *sign* is fixed in him or her more deeply than the tasks themselves. One has to live out that kind of pointing. And finally, this task can only be accomplished by pointing grace, which is shown all the more amazingly through our incapacity. There is no room for priests as a breed set apart.

Catholics and Protestants have traditionally disagreed over the Holy Eucharist and the role of the clergy who preside at it. Do we have anything to lift up? That has been the question. Do we have the capacity to offer up anything to God? Or is the movement, the sacrament, all downward—from God to us, as the Reformers insist? I am reminded of what the rabbis at the time of Jesus used to say: that when the messiah finally comes all of the sacrifices will fade away except one, the *todah*, the "sacrifice of praise and thanksgiving," to use Cranmer's term. For those who live by grace, depending entirely on what Jesus Christ has already done, this wonderful freedom from the burden of works elicits a sacrifice of praise and thanksgiving. What does that have to do with the coming life of a parish priest or pastor? The body of Christ is gathered around the world, and our task, by preaching and praying, is to issue a call to all of them to lift their hearts away from the details of their lives in celebration. We have to say to them, "Look, in the midst of your failings, sufferings, aspirations and blessings, Jesus Christ is really present here." And then, presiding at the table, we must point away from ourselves and away from them toward Christ alone, lest at any point we suppose that he is our present possession. We must point away, saying, "On the night *he* was betrayed, *he* took bread..." The Protestants are right—there is no offering of our own. Our task is only to point toward his self-oblation in and for the community. But the Catholics are right in this at least: that in issuing this call, week by week, our lives will be marked out, and by God's grace, given a "eucharistic shape." The purpose of the ordained ministry, in the future as well as in the present, is simply to remind congregations about the treasure *and* the clay and to do it "without confusion and without division," to borrow the famous words of Chalcedon. Clergy live to point like well-trained setters!

But what specifically will this pointing require of us? Who will engage in ordained ministry in these coming years and in our contemporary setting? To answer that question, I want to introduce you to four utterly hypothetical figures, and I want you to imagine them in a kind of mystery play—a tragi-comedy, if you will—in which we, wise as serpents and innocent as doves, must also act, and on whose plot the future fortunes of the ordained ministry in the church will turn.

First of all, I want to introduce to you Faith. She is a lax, lapsed parent. She has never come to church, and she knows next to nothing about the Bible, but since her baby came she has a sense that for the sake of the baby something ought to be done, a sense that is prodded in large measure by her equally lapsed mother-in law. She will knock at your office door, but she will balk at the ambitious string of "inquirers classes" that you developed in theological college. With half of yourself you will hold firm, remembering all that seminary talk about moving into a post-Constantinian age. The other half of your brain will whisper, "I can't teach her anything if she up and leaves for good." I heard those two voices for years as a parish priest. It is a battle that I fought with myself throughout my time in parish ministry—the arrival of the post-Christian era made tangible in the parish priest's life! Let us call this the challenge of *culture*. The best way I ever found to meet this challenge was to push those curious non-Christians as far as they would go through catechism. You spend your years in the parish slowly turning up the dial of intensity in catechism; you educate your lay leaders about what is at stake, and then you rest in all the grace God provides you. Get used to dealing with this tension throughout your entire ministry and be consoled that it is "meet and right"—this tension between the reality of a neo-pagan culture and the distinctiveness of the gospel *should* be there.

Second, I want to introduce to you Cyprian. He is the cutting-edge bishop, archdeacon or cardinal rector. (Here, lest I skate onto thin ice, I will speak only about my own experience in the United States with my own bishop!) Cyprian gets some things very right, and furthermore he is your friend. He has a concern for the poor, which is utterly valid. He does pray, and he reads from the same Bible and leads the same liturgy that you do. You like him personally; you do not doubt his sincerity, and you know that obedience is part of the call of Jesus Christ not only when you agree, but especially when you do not. The church is already too divided. And yet, not only on some secondary matters, but also on some big ones, Cyprian seems untethered by the word of God and seems to listen too much to the siren of the times. This is the challenge of *conflict*—not between the church and culture, but among the faithful themselves—and it will be your sidekick for much of your ministry. Paul exhorts us to speak the truth in love, the agape love that has to do, among other things, with the oneness of the church, and that spells a painful, costly kind of witnessing—one that preserves communion but does not paper over matters of truth. To be committed first to Jesus Christ, but to live out that commitment not in the abstract, but in a concrete community that sometimes errs, and to humbly keep the distinction between the treasure and the pot without separating them, so that you are "among sinners the first"—all this must be worked out day by day with much prayer and fasting, and most of all with a deep sense of patience and freedom, because in spite of all those struggles, Jesus Christ already reigns over his church.

Third, I want to introduce you to Ford. He is a consultant on church growth from the States. You can see your church demographics on the wall of your parish Columbarium, and you can see the cars in the community church down the street Sunday morning. You can hear your fellow Anglican clergy disparaging these church-growth seminars over donut holes in the clericus, but you can hear the worry behind their scorn as well. You know that the "wise scribe takes what is old and new," and that the children of Israel despoiled the Egyptians on the way to the Promised Land. And so you must borrow from the expert world of marketing. You have been helped by these seminars, and the people leading them are godly people. Yet there will be times when, with the best of motives, someone on your parish council will use the expression "market share," and it will make you itchy. Is this old-fogeyism? No, we have to borrow *and* to sift. We must bring in the harvest, and we are in a church that has neglected fruitfulness. Just the same, God's sense of size and time, whether of the mustard seed or of the wages of the latecomers, is strange. To borrow boldly, but also wisely and selectively, allowing the unique logic of the kingdom to prevail, this is the challenge of *consumerism*, and it will be before you as far as the eye can see.

Several years ago I got a piece of bulk mail, and it was addressed to "Fat George Sumner." I looked at the letter and I thought, "Well, I *have* had a few desserts recently, but I think this is excessive!" It turns out that "Fat" was an abbreviation for Father, and I had been a bit oversensitive. But the lesson is this: when you cut a reference to the clergy in half, they are a touchy crew!

This leads to our fourth challenge, whom I will refer to as Claire. Claire is the best warden you have ever had—or could hope for. She is devoted, and she has a strong faith. She is a highly competent professional whose spiritual life has been renewed in mid-life. She, like you, has caught hold of a vision for the ministry of every member of that parish, and she helps you offer discernment workshops, home Bible studies and lay schools of ministry. As a "womb to tomb" Anglican, this has been a breakthrough for her. But every once in a while, you worry that the collared baby might be going out with the bathwater. "Father knows best" was no good, but some unique role does remain. The trick, of course, is to avoid seeing your relationship to Claire and to the empowerment of lay ministry in opposition, to avoid thinking of them as some zero-sum game, but instead to think of what you are doing as the *condition* for the possibility of an awakened congregation. Let's call that the challenge of the *congregation* itself. In the diocese where I served before I came to Wycliffe College, they had discovered this theme of the ministry of the whole people of God, and in rural sections of the diocese they began a school of ministry. They made a list of all the potential ministries of the local congregation, of which presiding at the Eucharist was only one—so far, so good. But as I sat in a diocesan council listening to the list, I realized that a crucial piece of my life as a parish priest was missing. You see, they mentioned interceding and visiting, overseeing money, serving in the church and many different things—and all that was good. The gears were all there, but no one had listed the task of making sure the gears don't grind, of assuring that they do mesh. No one had the task of reminding the whole vehicle where it was going. The word rector means "straightener" or "orderer." This is not the same as the smoothing done by a dysfunctional "enabler," to use the parlance of the time. It does mean a ministry of traffic control and sometimes conflict mediation. Somebody has to enter in when warfare breaks out on the altar guild or in the choir room—and it will! Yet more importantly, you have to remind everyone why they are there—"for Christ's sake, and us as his servants," to quote St. Paul in 2 Corinthians. Rectoring is directing attention toward a goal: the prize of the upward call in Jesus Christ. In other words, good rectoring does not take the place of lay ministry, but it is "the condition for its possibility," to borrow an expression from the world of philosophy.

Hand over the ministries of serving and praying, witnessing and caring to your congregation decisively—but remember that they cannot perform those functions for long without you. You must pitch in to all those tangible ministries for your people, but you are really there for something different: pointing, praying, encouraging, occasionally admonishing and celebrating God's work. Your portfolio is less tangible, but it will demand everything you have. Claire and the congregation need strong, clear ministry more than ever, precisely because they are fully committed to lay ministry. In these most demanding times, you must live out—with fear and trembling—a reminder that we in the church have this treasure, but it is in clay pots.

How will you accomplish this more specifically? To that end, let us listen to our second Pauline word from 2 Timothy:

> I charge you therefore, before God, and the lordship of Christ, who will judge the living and the dead at his appearing in his kingdom. Preach the word. Be instant in season and out of season. Reprove, rebuke, exhort with all longsuffering and doctrine. For the time will come when they will not endure sound doctrine. But after their own lusts shall they heap to themselves teachers, having itching ears. They will turn away their ears from the truth, and shall be turned to fables. (2 Tim 4:1–4)

An analysis of the state of ministry today shows that the reigning model is a therapeutic one—that those who come to seminary, evangelicals included, do so with a desire to heal and along the way to be healed. The analysis goes on to say—and here I heartily agree—that all that is good, but it is not enough. No one is looking for a church that is "unpastoral," but the pastoral model is too inwardly focused, and so the new banner is "From maintenance to mission." That banner is appropriate—we do hope to send out into the church ordinands who have a zeal for evangelism. This change is thoroughly consistent with the idea of priest as pointer, because to remind the congregation that it has an obligation to those that have not heard is also to remind them that they exist not for the sake of the pot, but for the sake of the treasure, which is, after all, news. "Proclaim the message in season and out," says our reading. It is in this light that we can understand recent calls to render theological education more missional, more context-oriented, more outward-looking. May my mission professor's tongue cleave to the roof of my mouth if I say anything ill about all that! But given the time in which we will live and minister, that, too, is not enough. We who go out into the church will have to apply balm, and we will have to proclaim news, but we will also have to help them remember that news, that truth. We go forth as missionaries to a tribe of amnesiacs—they are as unlettered scripturally and credally as any German or Celtic tribesman faced by Boniface or Patrick. Our ministry must move from maintenance to mission—and I want to add a third *m*—to memory as well. For we go out as missionaries to a tribe of individualists, impatient devotees of the cult of self and "get" and "now." The German theologian Ingolf Dalforth recently said, "You must be missionaries to a deeply religious tribe, who believe that they will determine who God is."

By memory I do not mean stick-in-the-mud-ism. Pointing to the treasure amidst the clay will require creativity and challenge. To hear the word of God, with the creed as our guide, receptive to the wisdom of the fathers and the mothers of the church, seeing in our mind's eye the preceding line of holy martyrs—in an age like this, that is a radical challenge. To hold that we do not fabricate what we believe but receive it from God's hands by his grace—that is a subversive thought. Across the denominations, aided by the remembering of these truths, there is a growing "orthodox conspiracy" into which I invite you. It should be no surprise to those who study theology that Augustine heard Paul anew, and then Luther heard Paul with the aid of Augustine, and Barth heard the Scripture with the aid of Calvin, and the Caroline Divines of our own tradition had to hear the voice of the early fathers anew, and in our own time theology has been reinvigorated, not by some new idea, but by reclaiming the Trinity. We go to theological college not to devise our own theologies, nor to order up a brand of Christian spirituality from a course menu, but to be apprentices, rememberers, cherishers, indwellers, grateful recipients—and so the Holy Spirit will move and change the face of the church. It is by remembering and hearing again that the treasure gleams out in the midst of the clay.

In the parish I left in upstate New York, I lived among a number of "black bumper" Mennonites. One Lent we invited a group to our parish. Seated at a wonderful old country potluck, they issued to us what they called the Mennonite challenge—"This Lent, turn off your TVs and read one book of C. S. Lewis's every week!" You see, they were reading the great Anglican apologist and through him they called us back to our own theologically orthodox tradition, and thereby called into question our own consumerist assumptions. They told me how they drew lots to see who would be their pastor, assuming that everyone knew his or her Bible well enough, and how the first half of each of their sermons was an exposition given by the pastor, while the second half was an application to daily life given by the chief elder. We who advocate "total ministry" think we are talking about something on the cutting edge—the Mennonites have been living it for 400 years! Don't get me wrong—I'm fond of my car; my daughter is going to high school; and I do not expect the Anglican House of Bishops to be seen in black hats any time soon. But this much is true: the radical remembering of those Mennonites brought a challenge to us that spoke straight to the heart of our own cultural dilemmas and anxieties.

When I was in seminary the popular thing was to bring anthropological categories to bear on any subject. There was a kind of theological abdication in trying to explain to people that they were going to be something like shamans as they went out into the church. I do not think that is the way to go. Just the same, as a student of mission, I do want to give the insights of anthropology their due. The classic term here is *"liminal,"* a Latin word that means "a doorway," which was made popular by the anthropologist Victor Turner. Priests are doorways—but doorways between what and what? When thinking about the doorways between the divine and the human, we as Christians affirm with no doubt that there is one *liminal* figure: Jesus Christ. Still, in a weaker sense, one can say that clergy as I have imagined them, now and in the coming years, are twilight *liminal* figures. Our job is to stand betwixt and between things as they exist today in the church and things as they really are under the rule of the risen Jesus Christ. Our job is to point out the discrepancies and the commands that those discrepancies entail. We will be a doorway between seeing things in an everyday, humdrum way and the tremendous and mysterious vision of those same everyday realities in the company of the risen Jesus Christ. We must lead away from the centre, in the so-called realistic view, so that we can point to the real centre of all reality: the risen Jesus Christ. We have to remind congregations that the centre of their community, the door, is the one who was killed outside the wall. We must lead, exercising real authority and dealing wisely in real human dilemmas, so that our communities do not become cynical or hard-bitten. We have to exercise authority so that they remember, "It shall not be so among you." We, like all Christians, have to live in two places at once—in the already and the not yet—but we have to do it publicly, and in such a way that our struggles to do it edify and do not discourage. If all that is not *liminal,* I do not know what is.

My pickup is pulling into its destination, so here is my charge: in the coming years we have to make a careful distinction, upon which much depends, but which we and our congregations will often get wrong: we have to remind the evangelicals that the treasure is always in the pot and the Catholics that the treasure and the pot are not the same. Sometimes neither will want to hear us. We have to minister in a conflicted church in a de-Christianized age, standing for memory to the forgetful and for community to the individuals. No problem, right? Right. Because the church, creature of the Word, is a creature of grace, and the moment that we recognize its need is the moment when we spy on the horizon line the Spirit, and the Spirit's bright wings.

CHAPTER 4

ANGLICAN FORMATION
FOR MINISTRY

Victoria Matthews

I stand before you as living proof that the God we love and serve has a sense of humour—because I am an Anglo-Catholic woman in the episcopate speaking at an evangelical college conference on Anglican formation for ministry. At the recent House of Bishops' meeting one of the bishops asked me if I had heard the definitive argument that Jesus was a woman.

"Tell me," I beseeched him.

"It must be so," was the reply, "for she repeatedly fed thousands at a moment's notice; she spent three years trying to explain some pretty simple concepts to a group of men and finally, after she died and was buried, she rose again as there was work still to be done."

All joking aside, we do live at the crossroads where Christians of commitment and good conscience do battle over aspects of doctrine and Christian living that in living memory were thought to be universally understood and agreed upon. I am told the average length of time an Anglican priest presently serves in full-time ministry (stipendiary) is twenty-four years. That is the length of time we have been ordaining women to the presbyterate in Canada, and it is roughly double the length of time we have had the *Book of Alternative Services*. Twenty-four years ago the Anglican Church thought that formation for Anglican ministry was straightforward and defined. At Trinity College, Toronto, twenty-four years ago you didn't need to be male to study divinity, but every divinity student was automatically classed as "a man of college"—and no one really felt the need to change it.

When I was asked to address the topic, "Anglican Formation for Ministry," I quickly recognized that every descriptive word in that title had undergone a massive change in the last generation of leaders. Twenty-four years ago Anglicanism was not uniform but it was generally recognizable. There was no debate about lay presidency or the blessing of same-sex unions or the reception of the Eucharist by the unbaptized. Indeed we were only just discussing moving away from the norm of requiring the laying on of hands by the bishop in a service of confirmation as a prerequisite for reception of communion. Equally formation for ministry meant studying for ordination. Ministry was what the man in the black suit did and while ordination was required so was the three years in seminary (what the English frequently call the Vicar factory).

But while it is absolutely fair to say that there was greater clarity about ministry and Anglican formation for ministry, I am not sure that there was great clarity around faith and living out one's faith. Turn back the clock twenty to thirty years and the prophetic voice in our church isn't the first thing to catch your eye. Turn back the clock and you'd be hard pressed to find many parish churches with Bibles in the pews. Turn back the clock and you won't find anyone seriously talking about baptismal ministry.

The number of changes in our Anglican denomination has meant that many people are confused. Indeed it is reminiscent of a psychology experiment undertaken by Bruner and Postman. Those participating in the experiment were shown a pack of cards—one card at a time in fairly rapid succession. The task was to identify the cards as each was presented. However the pack of cards used had been altered. There was a *red* six of *spades* and a *black* four of *hearts,* etc.

Initially the altered cards were incorrectly identified while the other cards were easily recognized and named. But in time, for the exercise was repeated, even those easily identified cards caused confusion and the participants were virtually unable to proceed with the task. After still more time, most caught on, sharpened their wits and began naming what was presented absolutely accurately. But here's the interesting twist. I quote: "A few subjects, however, were never able to make the requisite adjustment of their categories. Even at forty times the average exposure required to recognize normal cards for what they were, more than 10% of the anomalous cards were not correctly identified." Acute personal distress was experienced as a result.

In recent years more than a few Anglicans have had difficulty recognizing the cards. When the way things have looked in the past changes, and we are confronted with a red—not black—six of spades, we are confused. In church land that may mean the altar being pulled out from the wall or it may mean being in the hospital and having a lay hospital visitor pay a call.

"Has the parish been in touch?"

"No, not yet—oh, yes, a nice lady came and prayed with me. She sings in the choir. But no one from the church so far."

The changes are many and varied: ordained women presiding at the sacraments, new Eucharistic prayers and the leader of another Christian denomination questioning the divinity of Christ. There is confusion and acute personal distress and sometimes it is no wonder that our church can't figure out what is of real importance and what isn't. Remember we are now talking about the Christian faith—and our salvation—and not playing cards.

In recent years the anomalies that have concerned us as Anglicans have had to do with doctrinal permanence and change, conflict and compatibility, unity and disunity in our faith. As the questions under debate increase, so does our distress—so much so that some Anglican seminaries see a major part of the curriculum as necessarily being dedicated to teaching tomorrow's leaders how to be agents of change and how to do conflict management. In J.M. Barrie's *Peter Pan,* Peter explains to Wendy that the lost boys are lost because they have no one to tell them stories. They cannot grow up because they have no stories to pass on to their children. Some would say that the Anglican Church has lost its way because we are no longer telling the Story: the Story of God's love and the salvation of the world. No wonder there is distress. Indeed when I read a prominent Anglican theologian, who I know is also read by countless lay people, and find that he is denying the Incarnation, Resurrection and the saving power of the Cross of Christ, I, too, know acute personal distress. Indeed the book has been thrown across the room! My distress is not that I don't have an answer, but for every well-informed Anglican reading the book there are twenty to a hundred who don't know the gospel and who will simply say, "That's really neat." Not knowing the story of salvation, any critique of it is convincing.

Let's leave that snapshot and focus the camera elsewhere. This time I would like to consider the place of our church and the place of our church leaders in society. Not many years ago clergy were held in esteem—equally so members of religious orders. It was assumed that we were of high moral character, learned and decent. With the scandal of Mount Cashel in Newfoundland, clergy have moved in public perception from being "moral" to at least being possibly deviant. There is no longer instant trust. There are windows in our office doors and understandably many dioceses require police checks for everyone in serious lay or ordained ministry. As an institution the situation in society has radically changed. The residential schools lawsuits have brought the churches again into the public eye. Although we participated and offered leadership because we were asked to do so by the federal government, we are being held accountable to a large degree for the policy of assimilation as well as the horrific and absolutely wrong acts of sexual and physical abuse. A very, very different example of how society's perception of the church has changed comes from the Diocese of Athabasca, where, following the Peace River flood, the Canadian Legion—but not the Anglican Church—was deemed an essential service and worthy of grant monies.

What does this have to do with formation for Anglican ministry? Quite a lot, interestingly enough. It means that those who are preparing for significant ministry in the Anglican and other mainline churches are joining a leadership body that is likely to be despised by a considerable percentage of the population. In many people's eyes we have become the "bad guys" in the "western" of life. For others we are useless, with nothing helpful or interesting to offer. "Father knows best" has become a somewhat humourous figure who is the unintentional comic and whose "help" frequently causes woe and disaster. Think of how clergy are portrayed by the entertainment media, and it is clear that we have been relegated to a category filled with those who live in a time warp.

One last snapshot of the society in which we live *vis à vis* the church. We hear a great deal about the spiritual hunger of the younger generation and their passing by of our churches to almost every other expression of faith and spirituality. I am acutely aware that we now have children in our communities whose parents have almost no Christian knowledge or faith. Generation X—the twenty- or thirty-something crowd who grew up (at least in the cities) with both parents working and a high rate of family breakdown—were the first generation to be almost totally absent from the churches. Perhaps because they were so familiar with father and mother in *absentia,* they never learned to relate to a heavenly parent—let alone God the Father, who is ever-present and caring. A wonderful layman in the Diocese of Edmonton was brought up short one day some fifteen years ago when his young son asked him who lived in the castle. The child was pointing towards a church and Ian realized he had done nothing whatsoever to introduce his son to God. Thanks to the grace of God and a fabulous parish, the family moved from total indifference to faithful Christian living.

It's that much harder for those under thirty-five to connect with the Christian faith because popular culture is infused with religious iconography and meaning. Many of us cringed when Andrew Lloyd Weber's musical *Joseph and the Amazing Technicolor Dreamcoat* had as one of its lead songs "Any Dream Will Do." Any dream? We also cringe, if we know about them, at the use of religious symbols in music videos. I offer a description of one such video by Tori Amos, entitled "Crucify:"

> "The interview fades [and] as it does, Amos speaks over two simultaneous images: a cross on a swinging chain in the foreground and the shadow of a birdcage in the background. In the birdcage stands what looks like a cross. The foreground cross swings lazily in slow motion.
> ...The cross, swinging on a chain (or is it a leash?), mesmerizes the viewer, suggesting that this cross, the institution's precious (metal) religious truth, hypnotizes its adherents." Tom Beaudoin, the author of *Virtual Faith* suggests this interpretation, after pointing out that Amos is the daughter of a Methodist minister. "To my reading, the images suggest that she has internalized (during her childhood?) this fetishized object of the Church, a golden bird that the Church keeps in its gilded cage. Artful and subtle, this is an attack on the Church as an institution that selfishly cages its glinting, dubious truth and hypnotizes its adherents with a gilded message. It is all brilliantly articulated in about ten seconds."

So you see, preparing for Anglican ministry is preparing for life in the trenches. Whether the challenge is from subtle changes in presentation (remember the experiment with the altered playing cards), or whether it is coming from coping and responding to the altered perception and decrease in trust of church leadership, the challenge is real. And finally the person preparing for Christian ministry needs to know and embrace a shift in calling. Anglican clergy can't be content with being chaplains. We need to be evangelists, interpreters of societal changes and a prophetic voice in the present age. And to do that we need to be steeped in the Christian tradition, people of faith and no stranger to secular society.

Let me move from the challenges facing those in the Anglican ministry now and in the future to what preparation/formation is needed for our future priests and leaders.

In brief I divide the areas of formation into: 1) devotional life (prayer and Scripture study); 2) knowledge and integration of the tradition through Scripture, church history, liturgy and theology (systematic, moral, etc.); 3) communication, evangelism, interpretation and pastoral care; 4) Christian morals and character (i.e., the gospel as transformation—gospel, culture and the prophetic voice).

The element, common throughout is, of course, integration and transformation. We need to become that which we proclaim. Of course we hand on that which we first received, but we never do that without changing ourselves—indeed, being transformed by what we receive. I am blessed to be in a diocese where many people make appointments to talk to me about pursuing theological education, ordination, specialized ministries, etc. What grace! Always, I ask about prayer life. (In fact, recently, when I've asked that question, people have laughed and said, "They said you'd ask that question and exactly how you'd ask it.") I don't pretend it's an original question. But frankly, if you are not spending a significant portion of time with God every day, seeking his will, experiencing his presence and engaging in adoration, praise, thanksgiving and intercession, why on earth do you think you should be more engaged in ministry? After all it's not our ministry, it's Christ's. To quote from 2 Corinthians 4: "For we do not proclaim ourselves; we proclaim Jesus Christ as Lord and ourselves as your slaves for Jesus' sake...we have this treasure in clay jars, so that it may be made clear that this extraordinary power belongs to God and does not come from us." We speak of Anglican formation for ministry because that is exactly what is needed. We need to be formed by God's grace. But formation doesn't happen in a vacuum. It requires real diligence on our part to place ourselves in God's hands. If you like, it is the responsibility of the clay to daily deliver itself into the hands of the potter. And the agency through which God in Christ in the power of the Spirit acts is, at least in part, prayer, the reading of Scripture and the Christian life. By the last of these I include that part of the ongoing formation for ministry that is self-examination and repentance: taking an honest look at one's life and seeking the grace and determination to change certain things. If your life is out of control and you are obese, addicted to alcohol or whatever, you need to address that before you start formal preparation for ministry. Why would someone think you have something to share that they want to listen to when your life looks like it needs saving?

The next on my list is what I call the tradition. The heart and soul of the tradition is Scripture, but Scripture didn't appear out of nowhere, nor does it live in a vacuum. The living tradition of the church is in the Word and witness of the good news of Jesus Christ. From the tradition we have received the revelation of the mystery of the holy and undivided Trinity; from tradition we know the lives of the saints (which is very important to the formation of which we speak, i.e., the making of saints). Jesus was raised in the Jewish tradition and knew the Scriptures. He knew them so well he could critique the practice of Judaism in his day.

In addition to serious and systematic Scripture study, I would love to see more emphasis placed on patristics—the study of Greek—and Anglican sacramental theology. I also need to say that sometimes the present-day teaching about the Trinity and Christology seems a bit lightweight. However, and here's the rub, you can't expect to receive a first-class theological education if when you enter you have a non-existent prayer life and you've never read the New Testament. You can't get into medical school without knowing the basic sciences, and I don't think the first year of divinity studies should have to be remedial Christian basics. It's easier said than done, because I know that we are failing our children and adolescents badly in our church schools and youth groups. We are so failing to form Christian disciples in our parishes that anyone who is interested in serious discipleship assumes the only route possible is to study theology at a university level—then, when they arrive there, they are quickly found to be biblically illiterate.

The third category is communication, interpretation and pastoral care. I include in this category evangelism and social justice/peace initiatives. If you are familiar with the *Book of Alternative Services* baptismal covenant, you will know that it first addresses belief— Trinitarian belief—in the declaration of faith we know as the Apostles' Creed. Then it asks the so-what question: so, what do you plan to do with this faith? Thus far we have addressed what St. Anselm called "faith seeking understanding," and that never stops in the Christian pilgrimage. But in addition to your own ongoing transformation, every Christian has the challenge of sharing and living the faith in the context of his or her life. It's true of the homemaker and brain surgeon, the artist, the student and the taxi driver. It is also true of ordained Anglican clergy and, in some respects, it may be even more difficult for us. Communication and interpretation has to do with discernment. As you enter a parish or conference or community event, you will need to be able to discern the sort of community that you will be joining and ideally to intuit your heart's desire. St. Augustine prayed, "God, you have made us for yourself and our hearts are restless until they find their rest in you."

C. S. Lewis said that people's discontent is usually misidentified, but we are not able to address that discontent until we also understand what they think they want. Twenty-five years ago when I was at Trinity College as an undergraduate, many of the men of the college dreamed about running away to the South Sea Islands. What they thought they wanted, of course, was wine, women and song— escape. C. S. Lewis would have us understand that they hungered after the Kingdom of God, not an earthly paradise, but these young men didn't know enough to identify their true hunger. It's rather like gorging oneself on junk food only to find that in place of hunger one now feels vaguely or acutely sick. So for ourselves: if we want to save the world, the first thing we need to realize is that it's already been done by the life, death and resurrection of Jesus. Our vocation, whatever it may be, is not to be the Saviour of the world! Our call is to communicate God's saving love in Christ and to help people identify their deepest hunger.

Communication, evangelism, interpretation and advocacy work all require us to understand the world in which we live. In many respects that means appreciating the different worlds experienced by a ninety-year-old in a care facility, a newly arrived refugee, an undergraduate and a line-worker in a factory. They do inhabit different worlds, and yet they all need the gospel that they may have life in all abundance. As everyone who has ever been either a student or a teacher knows, one learns best when the teacher evidences a personal interest in you and doesn't simply have knowledge, even saving knowledge, to impart.

I understand Cuddeston College in England requires its students to have one field placement that involves crossing cultural barriers. Their insight is that being a Christian minister in society means crossing the great divide between the extreme secularism and individuality of society and the gospel. When I finished my MDiv at Yale, I spent a few months in Haiti working with the Sisters of St. Margaret. Just before being ordained I'd realized that I'd had seven years of university but absolutely no firsthand experience of poverty. In Haiti I was embraced by people who had no earthly goods or security, but they did have a living, vibrant faith. In Haiti I experienced another conversion. I'd love to see formation for ministry include a three- or six- or twelve-month period in the developing world. We in North America have so much to learn from the people who live there.

Now I doubt you have been counting, but I have already outlined more than can be fitted into three years or twenty-one months or even twenty-eight months of study and field education, let alone allow the time for integration. I wonder, therefore, what would happen if we had entrance exams in Scripture and theology and liturgy, which every student had to pass before being admitted into divinity studies. I am a very strong believer that the study of divinity should show results. At the end of the three years it should be very evident that the student has spent time in the presence of God, but I'm not sure that can happen if the three years of the MDiv is a whirlwind of remedial Christian teaching so that one starts somewhere short of adequate confirmation preparation and ends up supposedly ready for serious ministry. One cannot grow a tree overnight, and I don't think Christian leadership is produced from a baptismal theory of "Just add water and stir."

Europe in recent decades has experienced the rise of lay communities. It is common for these young people to commit themselves to an hour of prayer and an hour of ministry with the poor every day. They know that one arises out of the other. They know they need to be confident that what they are doing is of God. They need to know that God is ever with them even as they seek to be obedient to God's will in difficult circumstances. That may sound fairly obvious, but I don't know where that sort of connecting of the spiritual life and the ministry of outreach is happening in present ministry formation. I certainly do not believe that it can happen when students are in isolation. Christian community needs to undergird prayer, study and the practice of ministry. As Jesus called together the twelve, he calls us into intentional community to be formed for ministry.

Thus far I haven't said anything about Christian morals and character other than that every Christian is called to a life of repentance. But let me be very clear about what I believe the church, our church, needs in her leaders. The present secular society has a rather smorgasbord approach to spirituality—a little of this, some of that and maybe a side order of something else. Construct your own religion to suit your own tastes. That is not the Christian faith. Jesus said, "Come, follow me," and he had strong words against those who put their hand to the plough only to change their mind. Much of the Christian world today knows firsthand what it is to suffer for the sake of Christ—but few first-world Anglicans do. Yet sacrifice, "take up your cross and follow me," is gospel teaching. And if following Christ means turning away from the ways and means of the dominant society—no sex outside of marriage, honesty and faithfulness in all things—such is the calling of every Christian. Anglican leaders in ministry need to embrace the high calling that is theirs in Christ. This isn't perfectionism, but it is discipleship. There are no Christian giants who are not also moral leaders.

My last word about formation is simply that I have high expectations of those who present themselves for ministry. But I also very much want them to have very high expectations of God, the Father, the Son and the Holy Spirit working in their own lives, working in and through Christian community—even high expectations of their bishop! Why? Because I truly believe we have become a church that assumes that nothing out of the ordinary will happen. We have forgotten the heritage of Acts 2:

> Awe came upon everyone, because many wonders and signs were being done by the apostles. All who believed were together and had all things in common; they would sell their possessions and goods and distribute the proceeds to all, as any had need. Day by day, as they spent much time together in the temple, they broke bread at home and ate their food with glad and generous hearts, praising God and having the goodwill of all the people. And day by day the Lord added to their number those who were being saved.

In a small way the healing ministry has revived expectations. But we are still a long way from living out George Carey's dictum, "Do great things for God and expect great things from God." It was another Archbishop of Canterbury, William Temple, who said, "It's odd, when I pray co-incidences happen; when I don't, they don't." We live in an age when people have more confidence in the power of coincidence (a.k.a., dumb luck) than in the power of God. Formation for Anglican ministry needs to be embraced by high expectations— faith in an all-powerful and all-loving God made incarnate in Jesus Christ. The call to ministry is the call to do what you know full well you cannot do save with the grace of God. "For God's foolishness is wiser than human wisdom, and God's weakness is stronger than human strength." "And remember, I am with you always, to the end of the age."

I cannot tell you to which expression of ministry God has called you in the Anglican Church, but I do believe you are called to radical discipleship, and that discipleship will take the shape and form to which you are called in Christ. God is the potter; you are the clay. Be molded, be formed into the very likeness of the crucified and risen Saviour. For it is in that formation, that discipleship, that you will know deep and abiding joy—your very heart's desire.

CHAPTER 5

WHAT I WISH I HAD KNOWN ABOUT MINISTRY WHEN I STARTED

Barry Parker

"Ho! Everyone who thirsts, come to the waters; and you that have no money come, buy and eat. Come, buy wine and milk without money and without cost. Why do you spend your money for that which is not bread, and your labor for that which does not satisfy? Listen carefully to me, and eat what is good, and delight yourselves in rich food. Incline your ear and come to me. Listen, so that you may live. …For my thoughts are not your thoughts, nor are your ways my ways," says the Lord. "For as the heavens are higher than the earth, so are my ways higher than your ways, my thoughts than your thoughts. For as the rain and the snow come down from the heavens, and do not return there until they have watered the earth, making it bring forth and sprout, giving seed to the sower and bread to the eater; so shall my word be that goes out from my mouth; it shall not return to me empty, but it shall accomplish that which

I purpose, and succeed in the thing for which I sent it." (Is 55: 1–3, 8–11)

The first book that I thought of when I was given this topic was *Everything I Needed to Know I Learned in Kindergarten* by Robert Fulghum. Given my own background, if I had to rewrite Fulghum's book, I would title it, *What I Needed to Learn in my First Five Years of Ministry, I Learned in Fire School.* My background is that of a firefighter and a paramedic, so I need to build a picture for you of what it was like for me to go to fire school the first time. Twenty-five years ago there was a group of young men—young "bucks"—out to save the world. We gathered the first day, and a training captain came in and surveyed this motley crew—strong and full of vinegar, ready to take on the world. He said, "Gentlemen, you all know what you're here for?"

"Oh, yes sir, we do," we responded.

"You're here to fight fires?" he asked.

"Yes, sir, we are."

"You're here to save lives?"

"Yes, sir, we are."

He said, "Well, welcome to my little part of hell."

It fit: fire school. We thought it was a joke, and we laughed uproariously, and away we went.

Out we went, first of all, for training. Imagine yourself as one of us. You do all sorts of exercises, but you live for the smokehouse, the day you first wear air-packs and you are sent in to rescue people. You are getting closer and closer to this big event. When the day comes, you dress in turn-out gear and air-packs, which are the bottles and the masks that firefighters wear, and you are ready. The smoke is billowing out of this three-story brick building. You know there is a dummy in there somewhere that you will be sent in—in teams of two—to find and to rescue, and you are on your way to becoming a real firefighter. Then they come along and say, "You have to change masks."

The mask that we get is the same, with one fundamental difference: instead of a clear plastic visor, there is only black plastic. When it goes on, you cannot see, and all you can hear is a lot of very loud noise. The training captain comes along and says, "Gentlemen, I told you what this would be like." It gets worse. He says, "My job, before I can let you loose on an unsuspecting public, is to disorient you as much as is humanly possible, so that absolutely nothing will deter you from what you have to do."

We learned the hard way what that meant: they had propane torches that they put very close to us so that we could feel the intense heat. You could hear people screaming!

The only way to train firefighters not to balk and back off is by going through the basics. I cannot tell you how many miles of hose I pumped, how many ladders I moved, how many knots I tied. We were the most disgruntled, depressed lot of young bucks you have ever seen, because we just wanted to go and save lives. In that short, singular experience of not being able to see, and experiencing what it's like to be *totally* disoriented, we had to go back and do the basics.

I would like to outline some of the basics for those who are entering ministry, those who are engaged in the early years of ministry and, with all due respect, those who have been at it a lot longer than I have. My ministry, in downtown Toronto, is certainly one of the most complex areas of ministry that I have encountered. One of the things that strikes me is that often the only thing I have to hold onto—I can say the Lord, no question—but more specifically it is that ability to go back to basics, to know that no matter how disoriented I am, there are certain fundamentals that will lead me through the smokehouse commonly called St. Paul's Bloor Street.

You have been hearing—and we all know it to be true—that there are so many things going on in the world around us and in the church in particular. The latest statistics show that the Anglican Church of Canada is losing—at least from denominational rolls—on the order of 18,000 members per year. No one is quite sure how accurate that number is. There is confusion over religious identity, and it has extended into the church with confusion about the identity of the presbyter. The presbyter wonders what he or she is there for. It is enhanced because of this one fundamental reality: in contemporary society the churches find themselves facing an institutional crisis, and the clergy person's role appears to be the hub around which so many of the problems facing the contemporary church are located. Here is the reason: "There's no profession on this planet," it has been written, "where the ideals, the values, the principles, and the professional commitment are so much part and parcel of one's work."[1] Doctors and lawyers are affected by their belief systems, but the work of the clergy *is* their belief system. Beliefs are the essence of "being," and for most ministers their work is their life. The distinction between getting one's value from *being* rather than from *doing* does not work here; ministers are "doing their being." When what you do is threatened or attacked, or it is going through an enormous dislocation and disorientation, it begs the question, who are you, as a minister of the gospel of Jesus Christ?

This drastic reorientation of the role—the role from which we as presbyters derive meaning—obviously causes some great dissonance and concern. It is truly an issue of being able, regardless of disorientation and dislocation, to be able to go back to those core things that make us who we are, because the role of ministry is inseparable from the person of the minister. The crisis of the church will immediately lead to personal crisis for the clergy *if* we stay caught up in roles that are constantly being hammered and buffeted in this day and age. There are all sorts of out-workings of that: stress and ambiguity, for example. To be a healthy pastor or presbyter—to stay alive in the midst of flame and fire—necessarily involves both external and internal expectations. It is my firm belief that we must be guided by a set of operating principles or beliefs that are authentic and contiguous with the gospel reality of a heart in tune with God. Therefore this is not an intellectual topic, per se; I am going quite blatantly and unapologetically for the heart, because our external behavior is contingent on our eternal heart.

The heart is the centre or focus of life, the spring of all desires, motives and moral choices—indeed, of all behaviors. Regardless of the emergencies that we keep hearing about in the church, regardless of the disorientation and dislocation that some of us have gone through—or, we know, will go through—it is important in this day of havoc that you and I understand what it is that we are about. Eugene Peterson, whom many of you know, wrote in his book *Working the Angles* something even more disturbing. It is bad enough that we catch it from the outside, but he starts talking about us presbyters from the inside! Peterson writes,

> The pastors are abandoning their posts left and right, at an alarming rate. They're not leaving their churches and getting other jobs; congregations still pay their salaries, their names remain on church stationery, and they continue to appear in pulpits on Sundays. But they are abandoning their posts, their calling. They have gone whoring after other gods. What they do with their time under the guise of pastoral ministry hasn't the remotest connection with what the church's pastors have done for most of twenty centuries.[2]

Now there is an indictment. Is it true? I cannot answer that for you, but I have to look at my own life and ministry.

Although roles are confused and the future uncertain—at least of the institutional church—here is my thesis: a core of clarity exists for the Christian pastor. Anglican clarity, regardless of what folks will tell us in our church, includes the identification of Scripture as the ultimate authority in matters of divine truth, spirituality, ethics and morals; a focus, both devotional and theological, on the person and work of Jesus, especially on his atoning work on the cross; and an emphasis on the transformative new birth as a life-changing, religious experience. Clarity in the present, I maintain, involves building Christian ministry on the things we know to be true, and it means that we have to do, first and foremost, some disciplined biblical exegesis. Much like our training captain told me years ago, that folding hose actually had a lot to do with saving lives. Knowing what the basics were—what you could trust to be true when everything else around you seemed untrustworthy, and even when fear just gnawed at your guts inside—you still had a way of staying the course.

So I want to begin exploring the basics outlined in Ephesians 4, the wonderful letter of grace to Ephesus, when Paul writes, "You are no longer strangers and aliens, but you are citizens with the saints, and also members of the household of God." In chapter four Paul talks about that wonderful issue of Christian unity, which has nothing to do with ecumenism or committees or officially sanctioned get-togethers, but states rather that we are united in the Spirit in the bond of peace. "There is one body and one Spirit, just as you were called to the one hope of your calling, one Lord, one faith, one baptism, one God and Father of all, who is above all, and through all, and in all" (v 4). He uses the word "one" seven times. I think he wants to send a message that the church is grounded in the unity of God—Father, Son and Holy Spirit. Therefore we have this incredible unity in the church—but in verse seven he launches into the great paradox of ministry: diversity in the unity. "But each of us was apportioned, or given grace, according to the measure of Christ's gift." Everyone in the church, in the body, has been apportioned from Christ himself. Grace. He then ties in a portion of Psalm 68 to remind us where that grace comes from—not from a structure, not from an ordinal, not from a college that granted us a degree, but from Christ himself—the one who ascended and descended, the one who is All in All, King of Kings, and Lord of Lords.

He gave those individual gifts to the church, but he also gave corporate gifts to churches—apostles, prophets and evangelists, who some have called "the obstetricians of the church," and also pastors and teachers, who are often called the pediatricians, the ones who are to raise baby Christians for this purpose: "To equip the saints, to make complete…" (v 12). The word *equip*, by the way, is used in Matthew 4:21 when the sons of Zebedee are mending their nets—they are repairing them, making them whole once again. The word "equip" means to make complete. The gift—the corporate gift—of pastor or teacher is to make complete the saints for the work of service, with the object of building up the body of Christ. Now, you can argue that with me. Bishop Victoria and I, having worked together, have argued that many times, and we have done it publicly, in the best sense of the word. I am not talking about the externals of churchmanship, but rather about what is the role description of the ordained presbyter, the pastor, teacher. There is the core.

What I want to suggest to you now is that there are some fundamentals—principles that you and I need to know in order to fulfill our roles. Forgive me if this is simplistic, but remember when Jesus said we must have a childlike faith? I am reduced, in the complexity of a huge congregation, to childlike status daily. I am reduced to this simple focus: what am I really there for? The first thing that is required in ministry, I believe, is knowledge of God—a good biblical theology. Second is knowledge of self, or realistic integrity. The third thing is knowledge of ministry, or role requirements. Knowledge here simply means "to confess, to recognize or admit as true." Confession is much different than just going, "Sure, why not? Whatever." Knowing God requires a biblical theology.

A controlling vision of ministry, life and theology is essential for the presbyter's inner health. A controlling vision is dependent first on knowing the reality of one's faith relationship with God the Father, God the Son and God the Holy Spirit. When I was in my first parish—and I was there for about a year—a nineteen-year-old man in our small community took his life. Those who are engaged in small-town ministry will know that often the whole community turns up for a funeral. It was to be held in the Elks' Hall, and they expected eight or nine hundred people, a good portion of our community. I went out to visit the family of this young man as they were getting ready to go to the funeral. His fifteen-year-old girlfriend was bouncing a two-year-old baby on her knee, and through the smoky haze and the bottles lined up she said to me, "Who are you and what do you do?"

I answered, "Well, I'm the minister."

She said, "Oh, and you're the guy who does the funeral thing?"

"Yeah."

"Well, you're not going to talk about God, are you?"

I said, "Why do you ask?"

She answered, "Well, nobody believes that [expletive] stuff anymore. Do you?"

In that one instant I was confronted with a question. What is my knowledge of God? Is it something I've been taught at seminary, read in Stott or Packer or Lewis, heard from Short or Robinson, or was it something that I truly believed? Thank God for the *Prayer Book* funeral service, because those words carried me and 950 other people through hell and back that day.

What is it that you know of God? Do you know him personally, through Jesus Christ, his Holy Spirit? Again, that might seem very simple to you, but I went through three years of seminary and no one bothered to ask me that—though I had to write papers on it. I could argue theology with the best of them. I knew about Jungian Christology; I could argue depth psychology and the great unconscious with anyone. Call it Christianity, but when it came down to my ultimate test of knowledge of God… Picture yourself standing by an open grave. Picture a worst-case scenario. For me, it is a murder within our family. Then look up at the faces gathered around this open grave—the family and friends of the person or child who is dead. Here is my question for you as ministers: what are you going to say, and what gives you the right to say it? What is your knowledge of God?

The second thing required in ministry is knowledge of self, or realistic integrity. This is one that can be perceived as self-serving, but it is absolutely essential that you and I know who we are before God. Not in a psychological sense, as people with or without great ego strength or self-focus, but rather that we are truly "Sinners in the Hands of an Angry God," that we are part of the creation, created in the image of God—but a very broken part of the creation. I am appalled and amazed, and I think it is absolutely ludicrous, when churches drop the confession because it does not fit the liturgy! I need the confession, because it is about the only thing that fits my life! Be honest—what do you know about yourself in relation to the Living God? He has created you uniquely as a child of his, yes, and all those good things. Without going to either polarity, or focusing on myself to the exclusion of others, or giving of myself to the exclusion of who I am as a man, a husband, a father, a friend and a pastor— what do I know about myself? What can I confess intimately? Self-differentiation is absolutely essential as a pastor. Self-differentiation, quite simply, means knowing that I am an *I* in relationship with *you*. It is knowing that you and I *count*, uniquely, both separately and together. However, we always maintain that knowledge in the context of our knowledge of God.

The last big core requirement for ministry is that you know ministry. I am always amazed that I went into ministry thinking that I knew what I would be doing because my dad had been a pastor. I spent most of my life trying to run away from that. People would say, "Are you going to grow up and be just like Dad?" My father, still living, is a wonderful man. He has been ordained for fifty-five years. He spent most of his early years in ministry coming to get me out of the principal's office after my numerous fights on the playground, because I had the only abnormal dad in my class. My classmates had farmers and factory workers and carpenters as fathers, but my dad wore black and talked to a guy you could not see. I reacted to this threatening situation like most young males. My father is now my best friend—I value his wisdom, I talk to him a few times a week, and I listen very carefully to what he has to tell me. Knowing who we are and what we are about, knowing the Living God—these include a knowledge of ministry that is not assumed. I want to highlight four things for you that I believe are absolutely essential for ordained, ordered ministry. The first is a "rule of life"—prayer, Scripture and discipline. The second is sustained proclamation of the Word through preaching. The third is the posture of the servant leader. Finally, the fourth is articulating and modeling the gospel.

Bishop Victoria has touched on the "rule of life." I certainly would not presume to tell an Anglo-Catholic about spiritual discipline. It is important; it is absolutely essential, especially the study of Scripture. I was told from early times to read my Bible, but no one told me to study it. I did something very interesting at St. Paul's Bloor Street: at every group I attended in the last month, I asked them the question, "If you could tell a baby priest like me what I need to know in the first five years of ministry, what would you say?" I can tell you this—if you want to know what ministry is about, ask folks in the pews. It was fascinating; it was a wonderful discussion. Every Bible study topic in the last two weeks has gone out the window because they wanted to talk about ministry, about what they wanted to hear. You know what? They want to hear from God, not from us. They can read the *Toronto Star* or the *Vancouver Sun* just as easily as we can. They don't want our opinion; they want to hear the Word of God. They want to know that God is real, not only in their lives, but in our lives as well. Scripture study, bathed in prayer, is the only way—I am absolutely convinced—that you and I will gain that knowledge.

The second item is something that I really want to focus on—sustained proclamation of the Word through preaching. Preaching is integral to the church—it is not an end in itself, but an important means to an end. As Paul said in his letter to the Corinthians, "For, since in the wisdom of God, the world did not know God through wisdom, so God decided [notice, *God* decided] through the foolishness of our proclamation, to save those who believe" (1 Cor 1:21). Preaching—and this is crucial—must first of all come from a theology that is rooted in firm convictions and from a bedrock of faith, because behind all preaching lies a composite conviction about God—his being, purpose and activity in the world. The folks in your congregation are going to hear your conviction about God, because it determines your preaching. You can tell them all the nice things about the Bible you want to tell, but if you do not believe that it is the Living Word of the Living God, they are going to know it. (It is also the enacted Word—in sacrament—and sung in hymns and embodied in the laying on of hands and other ministries.) As one who is finally learning this truth, I cannot stress enough that the primary thing necessary to preaching is a belief in the sufficiency of Scripture. When the sufficiency of Scripture is acknowledged, preaching becomes a very focused endeavor. The Bible contains the gospel, and therefore the best forms of preaching and teaching. Evangelism, pastoral care and ethical deliberations will all revolve around the authentic exposition of the Bible. Form or vehicle in preaching is secondary to sound biblical exposition, which is necessary to nurture and feed the individual and the community. I am told that Jonathan Edwards read his lengthy sermons in a monotone. A previous rector at St. Paul's Bloor Street allegedly preached his shortest sermon in fifty-seven minutes. Most of our services are done in fifty-seven minutes!

Preaching, though, is something more than just time or words. It is focus; focus on what must be done. Through the use of the Scriptures as the raw material of preaching, congregations will not only be taught and nurtured and brought to maturity in faith, but also equipped—remember, "made complete"—for effective ministry through the discipling thrust of Scripture. It is not simply oratory to your gathered congregation, but the formation of the church by God through his Word, as the Holy Spirit speaks through the Scriptures. The church, therefore, is dependent on the Word for its creation, existence and future hope. If we want to know where the church is going, then we need to proclaim the gospel of Jesus Christ, the whole counsel of God—not just the good parts. The good parts, my friends—at least what we think are the good parts—are killing us at the present time. Preaching is something that is learned. However, even Michael Ramsey, the great Anglo-Catholic Archbishop of Canterbury, said in his little book *The Christian Priest Today*:

> First, the priest is a teacher and preacher, and as such he is a man of theology. He is pledged to be a dedicated student of theology, and his study may not be vast in extent, but it will be deep in its integrity, not in order that it may be erudite, but in order that

it may be simple. It is those whose studies are shallow who are confused, and confusing.[3]

The theology of the presbyter is gained through prayer, Scripture and diligent study. When inadequate study is coupled with role conflict and ambiguity, the confusion is only enhanced. Then you are wandering around in the smokehouse, hitting your head on objects and not doing anyone any much good, even risking your own death.

There are elements, we know, that work against biblical preaching in the church today: the anti-authority mood in the culture, the technological revolution, the shift in communication and learning modes and perhaps, most acutely, the church's loss of confidence in the sufficiency of Scripture. I know all those things are out there, but if we believe what we say we believe, that Scripture is the Word of God, then our job is to be faithful to that. To proclaim the good news with integrity requires that the preacher is convinced about the reliability of the Scriptures. Preachers are called to preach the Word and to present the Word and to bring the Word directly to people. By definition, therefore, a sermon should not start with me as a preacher, with a subject, a theme or a gender bias. Rather, the sermon should begin with Scripture that contains the doctrine or theme that is required. Phillip Brooks himself said,

> "Truth through personality" is an acknowledgment that all of the faculties of the preacher must be brought to bear in a sermon. The total commitment of the preacher is required: mind, body, and spirit, for preaching is incarnational communication from God—prophetic, persuasive, and powerful.

Another quote, from J. I. Packer: "Personal clarity is therefore essential for the presbyter to preach effectively." I make this point as one whose preaching started off as storytelling. I was lauded in seminary because I am a good storyteller. I learned how to tell stories in the fire department—you can imagine what they were like. In fifteen years I have had a lot to repent of, and do you know how I learned? I had folks in the pews who would not settle for second best. I had folks who were saying, "You keep talking about the Word of God—where is it?" Our congregations have a lot to teach us. It has nothing to do with their roles or intellectual backgrounds. It has everything to do with their hunger for the Word, their desire for something that will transform their lives. I think our congregations know instinctively and spiritually when they are hearing that transforming Word. Some will not recognize it, of course; some will leave, and some will react.

The third thing that is essential in ministry is the posture of the servant leader. Leadership is exercised when an individual, by exhibiting a set of behaviors, influences a group towards the achievement of a common goal. The Ordinals expect the ordained clergy to function as leaders, for these services speak of the presbyter as one who fulfills the definition of "to lead": "to go with or ahead of, or show the way; to guide, to conduct, to serve." That definition is embodied in the Ordinals and certainly in Scripture.

Leadership in the church today can be about power, and so we need to study Jesus, study the Scriptures. When it comes to leadership, beware of what is out there in the marketplace. When I was working on my thesis I had to spend a lot of time reading all this stuff that is out there about management and leadership—and it is scary stuff, if you start to believe it. Again, go back in your Scripture study and in your prayers and stay with that core value that you know to be truth: that Jesus Christ came as a servant Lord—not as some entrepreneurial messiah to change the world by mail order, television or political and military means.

The leadership of Jesus is authoritative, spiritual and sacrificial; and as our ministry is an extension of his, so too is ours authoritative, spiritual and sacrificial. The servant leadership of the presbyter is crucial to the growth and effectiveness of the church, and the ultimate expression of this ministry is love for God and for one's neighbor as oneself. That love is the bond that holds all of ministry together in perfect harmony. The fundamental issues of leadership in ministry have been named as character and spiritual depth, qualities a person would associate with leadership. That essential core of servant leadership comes as a quest for Christian maturity. Even though it does not meet the world's agenda, this kingdom agenda must be served. Understanding God's purpose for the presbyter, and growing in one's awareness of the Holy Spirit, as he or she moves others in God's church, is really the heart of ministry. It is from this core that pastors can, with the utmost confidence, point to Jesus Christ as the Messiah, the Savior of the world, and the answer to the deepest human questions.

The proclamation ministry is motivated by Christian love, the outpouring of oneself, the agape of Christ's atoning work manifested in the preaching presbyter/leader. It is not formulaic, easy or even orderly; it is sloppy, hard grunt work. It is the work of faith, involving humans, self and others. The simplicity of prayerful servant love flies in the face of complex formulae and agendas. Many of you have probably been to conferences where there is some formula for leadership that will do it all. The simple reality is the sufficiency of Jesus Christ and his love shared in a broken world.

Leadership flows, then, from the Godly reality that the Christian leader must be true to self; ministry leadership is only meaningful when the leader is personally authentic and models this reality. It is easy to lose sight of servant leadership. The manager role, or the administrator role, can become overwhelming, even though they are only secondary things. It is easy for us to be waylaid, albeit with good and affirming tasks, and distracted from the core of ministry, from the essential nature of what we are called to do. It is easy to lose sight of the role of the presbyter in the parochial setting. But if we are to encourage and sustain movement toward the vision and mission that God supplies, presbyteral ministry must include a dimension that is tuned to the day of the Lord, the return of Jesus Christ. We lead people by loving, modeling, praying and proclaiming the vision of Christ in their midst.

However, we must foster an awareness of two extremes, which are ever-present dangers. The first is the danger that instead of making a

Godly vision permanent, and the specific goals changing, the vision becomes transient, while yesterday's goals remain permanent. The second is a familiar failing of visionaries and of people who live in the realm of ideas and issues: they are not inclined to soil their hands with the nuts and bolts of organizational function. For pastors, getting your hands dirty with your people, I believe, is absolutely essential. We need a balance of visionary direction-setting and practical out-working.

I want to highlight some key truths for servant leadership. Remember this: it is God's church. You will be under enormous pressure to make it your own—don't. I have a hard enough time fixing shelves in my house or changing the oil in my car. Why would I presume that the church was mine? It is God's church; his son, Jesus Christ, is the head, and we are the body of Christ himself. God's Holy Spirit empowers the church to fulfill its God-given mission and vision; presbyters are not the landlords of the church, but the stewards. Your leadership should reflect that reality.

Also, remember that all ministry begins with the individual Christian and is *rooted in the Christian community*. Christians are saved by the atoning work of Jesus Christ, and they are saved to serve. God's call to the presbyter to be a leader in the church is an outward and visible sign of his grace working in the person of that minister. A sense of belonging in ministry will be affirmed by the Christian community. A presbyteral leader with gifts and abilities firmly rooted in a biblical concept of servant ministry does not need to seek power through politics, personality or organization. The pressure of all these expectations—to be all things to all people—only leads to a debilitating clericalism through the delusion of omni-competence— that you can preach the Word of God like a Billy Graham and fix the sound system like Ralph the plumber. God has gifted each Christian with certain abilities, and he has gifted the body of Christ, his church, as Paul reminded us in Ephesians. A presbyteral leader has a responsibility to recognize, nurture and utilize all these God-given gifts to the glory of God and the care of our neighbor.

The presbyter does not have to bear the sins of the world either; that work has been completed. So often when I get caught up in things my wife comes alongside and whispers lovingly in my ear, "Remember, dear, we already have one Messiah; we do not need another." The pressure placed on the presbyter is truly to be all things to all people, to do even those things that we know, perhaps, are not right—or at least could wait. The servant ministry entails sharing burdens with people, not assuming burdens for them; the presbyter is not to be the equivalent of the Israelite scapegoat in Leviticus.

Finally, a continuing role in church leadership leads the presbyter to impart and enliven the vision of the church in a way that embodies integrity, dynamism and passion. Presbyteral leadership is intended to be life giving. It will serve by being directive or supportive, delegating whenever the situation requires it. Healthy leadership is not a static endeavor; it is authoritative, sacrificial and spiritual.

Finally, the fourth thing that is essential in ministry is articulating and modeling the gospel. John Wesley himself, when speaking at a conference in the eighteenth century, poses an essential question: "Ought not a minister to have, first, a good understanding, a clear apprehension, a sound judgement, and a capacity for reasoning with some closeness?" Wesley himself raises the importance of the ability to have some clarity about who God is in your life, who you are and what the roles of ministry are. Experience is essential, and you and I will grow in it. But the recovery of the vision for good, solid, presbyteral, Godly leadership has to be based on authentic principles of the Christian faith. Christian maturity will assume Christ as the centre, and everything flowing out from a solid foundation of biblical theology. "Without a stable and resolute core, truth disappears," says Carson, "retreating before the culture of interpretation, dissolving in the mists of postmodernity." Even though the prevailing culture mitigates against certainty of belief, especially belief rooted in objective reality and public truth, it is essential for the church to reclaim a place that has stability, roots and meaning—all growing out of biblical theology. A pastor's health requires an understanding of personal faith and its corporate expression. Integrity and congruency between the beliefs and the practice of ministry are essential; otherwise the uncertainty that flows from spiritual ambiguity will simply cause more dissonance, both internal and external. Assumption of belief implies, as Bishop Victoria said, integration of that belief.

I told you that I canvassed (and perhaps that is cheating, because pastors are supposed to know everything), asking folks who sit in the pews under my ministry what they wanted to see, not only in my ministry, but also in the ministry of someone coming in for the first time. Here is a synopsis of the answers from a broad range of folks to the question, "What is required in the first five years of ministry?" Their answers convey what I wish I had known in the first five years of ministry, and what I pray I will be able to live out to the end of my ministry. First, the *Word* of God changes and transforms—neither the minister, the liturgy nor the church have the power to transform us. Second, do not assume the gospel: preach it, teach it, live it. Third, genuine transparency is absolutely essential; be viciously honest with yourself and before God. Fourth, know what you do not know—and admit it. Fifth, be a life and linguistic translator; know how to speak the language of the people that God has placed in your care, and in whose care you have been placed. I speak to firefighters differently, when I am evangelizing them in a pub, than I speak at St. Paul's Bloor Street on a Sunday morning, or with the street people that we feed every Wednesday. Know the language of the people—much like Paul did at the Aereopagus. Know the context; be able to translate. Sixth, the plea of lay people is, "Know what you are for." They do not want to keep hearing what you are against. It is safe to say that you are for Jesus. Seventh, focus on significance rather than success—this is a growing issue. We have a lot of very wealthy "significant folks" in our congregation, but as you start to unpeel the layers, you learn that success is not the issue, but rather significance. The Bible has a lot to say about that. Eighth, one of the issues that people are wrestling with is how to understand evil in their midst, and they feel the church does not take this seriously enough.

Ministry is not about what God is doing; it is rooted in who God is. When you know who he is, you can see what he is doing. The *Book of Common Prayer* acknowledges that in the Ordinal, of course, in those wonderful biblical metaphors of shepherd, messenger, watchman and steward. Be an equipper, as Paul says in Ephesians 4, rather than a facilitator, sharer, dialoguer or whatever we are supposed to be today. Also, know what your passions are, what you feel really strongly about. If you believe in Jesus Christ, then for heaven's sake, be passionate. He was passionate enough to die for us; the least we can do is to speak passionately about him. I was taught, as an Anglican, to do everything decently and in good order. It has been said, "Well the charismatic renewal movement came along and fixed all that," but that is not true. Your passions do not depend on whether you are a "Type A" extrovert off the map, like I am, or whether you are a quiet, introspective, studious person. That is not what I am talking about. I am talking about a passion and a heart for the gospel of Jesus Christ. We can talk about the church, ministry, parishes and all sorts of stuff, but if you have no passion, then you have to ask yourself what you know about God, what you know about yourself, and what you know about ministry. You and I have the incredible privilege—ordained or not—that when we said, "Yes" to Jesus Christ, we were given the opportunity to serve in his name. We can serve in so many different ways. My plea for you, as one who has had to come to grips with the Living God—simply because he came to grips with me—is to share your passion with others, to let them know what you believe, to be honest about what you are not sure of, to be the one to proclaim the whole counsel of God, to trust the sufficiency of Scripture and to know that Jesus Christ did something remarkable on the cross—not just something optional.

ENDNOTES

1. Paddy Ducklow, "Dear Church! We Quit!" *Crux* 31:2 (June 1992), 32.

2. Eugene H. Peterson, *Working the Angles: The Shape of Pastoral Integrity* (Grand Rapids: Eerdmans, 1993), 1.

3. Michael Ramsey, *The Christian Priest Today* (London: SPCK, 1972), 7.

4. "Brooks, Phillips" as in Reid, Daniel G., Robert D. Linder, Bruce L. Shelley, and Harry S. Stout, ed. *Dictionary of Christianity in America* (Downers Grove, IL: InterVarsity Press, 1990).

CHAPTER 6

SELF-CARE FOR PASTORS: RICHES FROM THE ANGLICAN DEVOTIONAL TRADITION

J.I. Packer

L ook after yourself," my parents would say as, back in Britain in my youth, I would take off for some youth hostelling. "Take care" is what we all say nowadays in North America as we wish each other goodbye. A decade ago in the USA a book titled *Care of the Soul* became a best-seller. Such care—care for oneself, keeping in good personal shape and performing well—is my theme now, and I shall explore it, or try to, in fully Christian terms.

The self-care that I shall seek to promote is not care for oneself by oneself, as if keeping spiritually healthy is a solo venture. In real Christianity that is never so. Just as it is not good sense for a physician to try to be his own doctor or a dentist to try to fill his own teeth, so in Christian life and ministry it is not wise—nor therefore is it right—to attempt the practice of self-sufficiency. All Christians need the help of others—that is the essence of fellowship, after all—and pastors, so I urge, need this mutuality of care more than most. This is a matter about which the churches of the West are becoming increasingly concerned as pastor after pastor collapses through moral weakness, breakdown or burnout. Our historic habit of idolizing pastors and placing them on pedestals isolates them and makes them very vulnerable in all sorts of ways. That some form of peer fellowship with mentoring, direction and accountability needs to be in place for all pastors is, for the purposes of this essay, a given. My present task is to offer soundings in the rich heritage of Anglican wisdom for the refreshing and enriching of pastors in their daily work. The Anglican pastoral tradition is a noble one, and it has left us much vitamin-laden literature, and the pick-me-up effect of devotional reading in this field can be marvelously strong. So to all clergy and would-be clergy I say at the outset: over and above seeking the fellowship you need, get into this literature. It has thrilled me and done me good, and I am bold to predict that it will do the same for you.

Before going further, let me reflect on some of the realities of ministry today. The demands of presbyterial servant-leadership have never been greater, nor more perplexing and disorienting, than they are in the modern West today. We serve in a changing and, frankly, lurching church and in a society that is busy marginalizing Christianity. In place of old-fashioned respect and attention, we clergy constantly find ourselves facing suspicion and contempt, ignorance and unconcern about what we stand for, and a readiness to laugh it off—indeed, sneer it off—if we make the attempt, as they say, to strut our Christian stuff. Most people around us still believe in God, but they see the church and active Christian commitment as among life's irrelevances. Is this likely to change? Seemingly, no.

The backlash of this is jolting. Because the personal identity of the clergy is so closely bound up with their public ministry, disrespect for the latter is felt as a kind of threat to the former. Of all the professions, that of the pastor has become the one requiring the largest investment of creative thought and resourceful energy—and the one yielding least return, in the short-term at any rate, on this investment. Perhaps it was ever thus: Jesus himself said that one sows and another reaps. Maybe, then, yesterday's spectacular ministries, expanding small congregations and turning large ones around, were always the exception rather than the rule. But at all events it is so now, and the possibilities of discouragement, disillusionment and bitterness, even of broken-heartedness, in this situation are huge.

Satan will go on stirring up the world's hostility toward the church; the book of Revelation shows that. And if he cannot keep people out of God's church and kingdom, he will do all he can to ensure that they well and truly dishonour him from within the fellowship; the letters to the Galatians, the Corinthians and six of the seven churches in Asia Minor, not to mention the pastoral epistles, show that. So clergy with clear principles may find themselves opposed and under threat from their flock at any time, even to the point of their termination—as happened to Jonathan Edwards, champion of the Great Awakening, channel of revival to his own people, the best brain in the American colonies of his day, when he set himself to establish the rule that only accredited believers, as distinct from mere well-wishers to the faith, might come to the Lord's Table. Because this would have raised the bar for church membership and embarrassed regular communicants who did not profess conversion, the congregation threw Edwards out. Ministers who move things forward regularly risk rebellion in the ranks, prompted not by spiritual insight but by love of the familiar backed by Satan's love of setting Christians at each others' throats. We must be realistic about this.

Now it is clear why it is wise to tell people thinking of ordained ministry that they should keep out of it if God will let them. If they can live with a clear conscience while serving God in other roles, they should do so. If they are only volunteers, in the spirit of the world's do-gooders, they will lack the compelling sense of call that enables pastors to stand up to the perversities and pressures that they must face.

Clear also is the need for all pastors to be in good spiritual health at all times. Everyone nowadays recognizes the importance of good physical health, and we give time and trouble to achieve and maintain it. It is equally important that the church's leaders be spiritually healthy and order their lives to this end—though this need is sometimes overlooked by both congregations and pastors. Bodily health, we know, requires food, sleep and exercise, plus a way of living that is free from destructive habits, addictions to harmful things, substance abuse and such like. Surface-level correspondences with requirements for spiritual health, in pastors as in other Christians, are easy to see. Matching nourishment through food is a diet of Holy Scripture read, marked, learned and inwardly digested, with appropriate additional reading to advance understanding of what Scripture means and how it applies. Matching refreshment through sleep is the proportioned rhythm of life that keeps professional and voluntary church work, family times, hobbies and whatever else in a balance that suits our make-up and ensures that exhausting exertion is followed by relaxations and recreative activities that reinvigorate mind and heart. Matching physical exertion is the discipline of regularly using God's appointed means of grace—meditation, prayer, worship, fellowship. Matching avoidance of habits that harm the body is the necessary life-watch against sin in all its forms—unfaith, unlove, pride, envy, lust, hate and so on. Woe betide the Christian, and doubly so the pastor, who neglects the rules of spiritual health at any of these points.

But there is more to be said than this. We must sharpen the focus and go deeper. Rival accounts of the Christian life are on offer, and it is vital that real Christian existence according to the New Testament should be clearly understood and explicitly embraced. The paragraphs that follow, therefore, are crucially significant. The basic reality in the Christian life is the forgiveness of sins understood in New Testament terms: namely, as the decisive relational change called justification by faith, the truth that Luther labeled the "wonderful exchange." The glorious reality here is that because the incarnate Christ, mankind's representative, took our sins and bore them in our place on the cross, those who now put faith in him as risen Saviour and Lord enter into a new relationship with God, one of pardon, peace, acceptance, adoption and assurance of faith and hope, a relationship mirroring nothing less than the Father's full, eternal, unqualified embrace of the Son in endless love and joy. Justification is God's final word on where believers will spend eternity, and reaffirmation of this—our blood-bought privilege—is his daily response to our daily confessing of new sins and pleading for renewed pardon. In Peter's words, Christ "suffered once for sins, the righteous for the unrighteous, that he might bring us to God" (1 Pt 3:18), so that now, as John says, "our fellowship is with the Father and with his Son Jesus Christ" (1 Jn 1: 3). Paul puts it thus: God "made him to be sin who knew no sin, that in him we might become the righteousness of God" (2 Cor 5:21).

Wonderful as this relational change is, however, it is not the whole of our salvation; indeed, from one standpoint, it is not even half of it—just as the foundation, however firm, is not even half the house that rests on it. With our altered status comes an altered state. Those who put their trust for life and salvation in the Lord Jesus are, in a mysterious way that passes our understanding, united with him in his risen life by the Holy Spirit: co-resurrected with him in him, says Paul (Rom 6:5; Eph 2:4–7; Col 2:12–13); born again of God by the Spirit in a life-changing way, say Jesus and John (Jn 3:3–8; 1 Jn 3:9). Their heart—that is, in Bible usage, the motivational core and centre of their personal being, their deepest consciousness and the deeper reality that shapes it—is re-created and transformed, so that their actual living begins to become attitudinally and actively Christ-like. Re-creation—new creation, making us into what before we were not—is how Paul theologizes this change in 2 Corinthians 5: 17–18, where he gains emphasis by omitting the verb and so turning what would otherwise have been a statement into an exclamation: "If anyone is in Christ—new creation! The old has passed away; behold, the new has come!" The "new" is that of which Paul spoke in verse 15, namely "that those who live might no longer live for themselves, but for him who for their sake died and was raised." This states not only God's goal but also his achievement, for the essence of the "new" is that henceforth the driving desire of each believer's heart is to love, serve, honour, exalt, magnify, glorify, obey and please the Father and the Son. This desire is recognizably an embryonic reproduction of the desire that has been driving the Son of God in his relationship to the Father before, during and since his life on earth. A person would not be regenerate at all were this desire not present within.

So the self-centered, narcissistic life that believers lived before their new birth is finished, for in the most literal theological sense, they have no heart for it any more. We who believe have been crucified with Christ and baptized into his death (Gal 2:20; Rom 6:4–13); in that sense we have truly died, and our life—that is, our new life, our risen life in Christ—is hidden with Christ in God (Col 3:3). That life is the dynamic of a new moral energy in and from our heart. To be sure, sin, which ruled us before, now dethroned in our heart but not yet destroyed in our lives, remains a distracting and disfiguring force in our spiritual system. Watching against it, resisting its manifold urges and mortifying it (putting it to death, that is, by draining away its life—note the use of the Greek verbs *thanatoō* [Rom 8:14] and *nekroō* [Col 3: 5], which both mean to turn a living reality into a corpse) has to be a sustained struggle as long as we are in this world. But the momentous thing happening throughout (not that we can always see it) is that God is actively transforming us toward the full moral likeness of our Lord; and in this he works from the inside out, starting with desires of the heart and purposes of the mind, which he leads us to express in action in a process that Paul describes as being changed from one degree of glory to another by the Spirit of the Lord (2 Cor 3:18). The process is, indeed—to Paul's way of thinking—glorification as such already begun (cf. Rom 8:30).

I state this at some length, not only because it is the basic truth about the Christian life—of the clergy as well as of all others—but also because, familiar as this doctrine was from the seventeenth to the nineteenth century, among today's Protestant Christians it is largely unknown country. I have found that when I teach about Christian living I have to start here, or people never become realistic about what goes on inside them, nor do they grasp how God is preparing us for the glory that is to be. We here encounter a twenty-first-century blind spot.

Much of what is involved in what I am saying can be expressed by calling the real Christian life the baptismal life, in the sense that the symbolism of going under water, which signifies dying with Christ to all that one's life was before, followed then by coming up and out from under, which signifies rising to share the present, permanent life of the risen Saviour, mirrors the constantly recurring emotional shape of Christian experience. Over and over in God's providence, Christians (and pastors perhaps more than any) have experiences that feel like death—loss, rejection, ill-treatment, isolation, failure, relational breakdown, collapse of plans, pain, grief, weakness, burnout, inability to help, feeling out of one's depth, swamped and drained, brought to the end of oneself and one's own resources. And then God in mercy lifts us up into what may fairly be called a resurrection experience, in which we find that with God as our upholder we are unsinkable after all. In 2 Corinthians 1:8–10, Paul writes,

> we were so utterly burdened beyond our strength that we despaired of life itself. Indeed, we felt that we had received the sentence of death. But that was to make us rely not on ourselves but on God who raises the dead. He delivered us from such a deadly peril, and he will deliver us.

This—with much else in that letter, as Paul in conscious bodily weakness shares himself with converts who brush him off—is a full-dress example of the baptismal life as pastors in particular repeatedly experience it. But this pattern is constantly at the heart of every real Christian's inner life.

Two corollaries for pastors and others, both leaders and followers, must be noted here. First, our Christian living must be *disciplined,* and the discipline should take the form of practicing the moral and spiritual habits on which many books have been written since Richard Foster published *Celebration of Discipline* in 1978. Of these books the best I know is Donald Whitney's *Spiritual Disciplines for the Christian*

Life (NavPress, 1991). *The Book of Common Prayer* is rarely viewed as a manual of devotional discipline, but used thoughtfully on a day-to-day basis, it becomes as good a one as you will find. A lady I knew in my youth, who was middle-aged when Queen Victoria died, would withdraw daily for her devotions with a Bible and a Prayer Book in her hand. She could hardly have done better, and many I have known since have not done so well.

Second, our Christian living must be *dependent*, not only on our God but also on our fellow Christians, or we shall surely come short. Yesterday's fellow Christians minister to us by the writings and example they have left us; today's fellow believers minister to us by friendship, support and committed prayer. We were not made, nor are we redeemed, for self-sufficiency, and when John Wesley declared that there is nothing more un-Christian than a solitary Christian he was right on target. At theological college I was told that a clergyperson should not have friends in the congregation and should budget for a fairly isolated life all the time. The purpose of this advice was to rule out favoritism, but I now think it was fundamentally wrong-headed. Not only is it true, at least in my opinion, that as the pastor pastors the congregation, so the congregation should pastor the pastor, through the lay leaders with whom he works or the peers and veterans whom he finds in the flock; but most clergypersons' well-being spiritually now seems to me to be largely dependent on this happening.

The Puritans held that every Christian needs a "bosom friend," as David and Jonathan were bosom friends. The phrase means a person with whom one practices what we nowadays call mutual accountability, a committed concern for the spiritual state of one's friend as well as other aspects of his or her life. Often called "soul-friends," such persons do informally for each other what spiritual directors and confessors do in an institutional frame. Every Christian, so it seems to me, needs at least one soul-friend relationship, and pastors most of all.

Any survey of real Christian life must take note of the constant, inescapable battles that have to be fought against spiritual degeneracy in the form of unbelief of God's Word, unforgiveness of other people and unhumbled pride in what we are and have done. These are three main avenues of Satanic attack on leaders as on others.

In these days of liberal Christianity in our churches and post-Christianity in the culture outside, unbelief of God's affirmations in the Bible and the gospel is rife. Justification by faith (Luther's *simul justus et peccator,* being accepted by God while yet a sinner) is not understood, divine promises are not received and trusted, and Christians fed on liberal teaching flounder. Unforgiveness, which is a form of unlove, is regularly an expression of hurt pride and resentment, disguised as self-respect. As Jesus often warned (Mt 6: 14–15; 18:21–35; Mk 11:25; Lk 6:37), unforgiveness is a total block to the blessing of God. Unhumbled pride, as is often said, takes four forms: pride of face, when you think you are most handsome; pride of race, when you think your skin is the best colour; pride of place, when you think you are better positioned than others; and pride of grace, when you think you are one of God's top people—and pride of grace is the worst of the lot. All these forms of spiritual degeneration banish true spiritual joy—which for healthy believers is constant—and create pitfalls for pastors in abundance.

Such, then, in outline is the real Christian life of fellowship with the Father and the Son in faith, hope and love. It is this life that believers as such, and pastors in particular, are called to live. And devotional reading will only do us good as we set ourselves to order our lives in these terms.

But, given that, I propose now to present to you five longtime friends of mine, all celebrities of the Anglican past, whom I call friends because of the devotional benefit they have brought me. I am not saying that they are the only Anglican exponents of Christian communion with God that are worth reading (that would be grossly false); I simply say that they have helped me in specific ways, and I think and hope they may help you similarly. So I want to tell you about them.

I should add, before going further, that I estimate all these five as evangelicals in the generic sense of being sufficiently clear on the realities of salvation that the previous pages have sought to spell out. Luminaries like Jeremy Taylor and William Law, to name just two, do not make my list because, however strong they are at other points, their clarity here is less discernible, at least to me.

First, I speak of William Perkins, the C. S. Lewis of Elizabethan Puritanism, who died in his forties in 1602, while Elizabeth I was still queen. He was a Cambridge don who produced a series of benchmark popular manuals laying out Puritan practical wisdom for living the Christian life. In this pioneer enterprise he was always clear, masterful, businesslike and searching; his books met a felt need and circulated widely. In *A Graine of Musterd-seede* (1597) Perkins argues that the beginnings of spiritual life in the soul prove themselves genuine not by any form of intrinsic intensity but by leading on to progress and growth in grace, and he offers guidelines for those who wish to grow spiritually in which the later wisdom of Brother Lawrence on practicing the presence of God is strikingly anticipated. Here are the high spots of his nineteen points:

1. In what place soever thou art, whether alone or abroad, by day or by night, and whatsoever thou art doing, set thyself in the presence of God. Let this persuasion always take place in thy heart, that thou art before the living God: and do thy endeavour that this persuasion may smite thy heart with awe and reverence, and make thee afraid to sin. This counsel the Lord gave Abraham [Gen 17:1]...

2. Esteem of every present day as the day of thy death: and therefore live as though thou wert dying and do those good duties every day, that thou wouldst do if thou wert dying. This is Christian watchfulness.

3. Make catalogues…of thine own sins, specially of those sins that have most dishonoured God and wounded thine own conscience. Set them before thee often, specially then when thou hast any particular occasion of renewing thy repentance… [Thus, says Perkins, one fulfils the biblical pattern of considering one's ways, confessing one's past sins and correcting one's course of life: Pss 25, 119:59.]

4. When thou first openest thine eyes in the morning, pray to God and give him thanks heartily. God shall then have his honour and thy heart shall be the better for it the whole day following…And when thou liest down, let that [i.e., prayer and thanks] be the last also, for thou knowest not whether fallen asleep, thou shalt ever rise again alive.

5. Labour to see and feel thy spiritual poverty…specially those inward corruptions of unbelief, pride, self-love, etc.…that…if thou be demanded what is the best thing in the world for thee, thy heart and conscience may answer with a loud and strong cry, "One drop of the blood of Christ to wash away my sins."

6. Show thyself to be a member of Christ and a servant of God every day.

7. Search the Scriptures to see what is sin and what is not sin in every action. This done, carry in thy heart a constant and resolute purpose not to sin in anything, for faith and the purpose of sinning can never stand together.

15. Make conscience of idle, vain, unhonest and ungodly thoughts, for these are the seeds and beginnings of actual sin in word and deed. [Uncontrolled wandering thoughts, so Perkins warns us, *always* wander into a bad place!] The want of care in ordering and composing our thoughts is often punished with a fearful temptations in the very thought…

16. Cleave not by inordinate affection to any creature, but above all things quiet and rest thy mind in Christ; above all dignity and honour, above....all health and beauty, above all joy and delight, above all fame and praise, above all mirth and consolation that man's heart can feel or devise beside Christ.[1]

And so on. Perkins offers it all as wisdom for all, which indeed it is; but it is wisdom for clergypersons supremely. For the dictum of the Scottish pastor Murray McCheyne remains true for all congregational leaders: "My people's greatest need is my personal holiness."

I move on to a later Puritan, Richard Baxter, who was Episcopally ordained in 1638. Baxter only wanted to be a parish minister of the national church, but the 1662 Act of Uniformity made him a nonconformist. In less than fifteen years (before 1662), he virtually converted the English Midlands town of Kidderminster. He is perhaps the foremost, as he is certainly the most voluminous, of Puritan practical writers. He wrote his *Reformed Pastor* ("Reformed" meaning what we would express by saying "revived") in 1656 to arouse and admonish a clerical fraternity (the Worcestershire Association) that was covenanting to catechize families in their homes on a regular basis, and the book was described by Bishop H. Hensley Henson in 1925 as "the best model of the clergyman's duty in the language, because it leaves on the reader's mind an ineffaceable impression of the sublimity and awefulness ['awesomeness' is what we should say] of spiritual ministry."[2] Here are two extracts that speak to me of my self-care as a pastor, which I want to share with you.

Be also careful that your graces are kept in vigorous and lively exercise, and that you preach to yourselves the sermons which you study, before you preach them to others...When your minds are in a holy, heavenly frame, your people are likely to partake of the fruits of it...that which is most on your hearts is like to be most in their ears. I confess I must speak it by lamentable experience, that I publish to my flock the distempers of my own soul...We are the nurses of Christ's little ones. If we forbear taking food ourselves, we shall famish them...If we let our love decline, we are not like to raise up theirs. If we abate our holy care and fear, it will appear in our preaching…Whereas, if we abound in faith, and love, and zeal, how would it overflow to the refreshing of our congregations, and how would it appear in the increase of the same graces in them! O brethren, watch therefore over your own hearts: keep out lusts and passions, and worldly inclinations; keep up the life of faith, and love, and zeal; be much at home, and much with God.[3]

And now this:

He must not be himself a babe in knowledge, that will teach men all these mysterious things which must be known in order to salvation… O what strongholds have we to batter, and how many of them! What subtle and obstinate resistance must we expect from every heart we deal with! …We cannot make a breach in their groundless hopes and carnal peace, but they have twenty shifts and seeming reasons to make it up again; and twenty enemies, that are seeming friends, are ready to help them…We have wilful, unreasonable people to deal with, who, when they are silenced, are never the more convinced… We have not one, but multitudes of raging passions…to dispute against at once, whenever we go about the conversion of a sinner…As Peter saith to every Christian, in consideration of our great approaching change, "What manner of persons ought we to be in all holy conversation and godliness!" so may I say to every minister, "Seeing all these things lie upon our hands, what manner of persons ought we to be in all holy endeavours and resolutions for our work!" This is not a burden for the shoulders of a child…To preach a sermon, I think, is not the hardest part; and yet what skill is necessary to make the truth plain; to convince the hearers, to let irresistible light into their consciences, and to keep it there, and drive all home; to screw the truth into their minds, and work Christ into their affections; …to drive sinners to a stand, and make them see that there is no hope, but that they must unavoidably be either converted or condemned…How many sleep under us, because our hearts and tongues are sleepy, and we bring not with us so much skill and zeal as to awake them![4]

As the wise Christian will re-read Bunyan's *Pilgrim's Progress* annually, so the wise pastor will add to that a journey each year through Baxter's *Reformed Pastor.*

George Whitefield (1714–70) is the third friend whom I wish to share with you. Pioneer of the eighteenth-century revival in just about all its aspects on both sides of the Atlantic, he was a sunny, straightforward Church of England clergyman hugely endowed with the communicative gifts and instincts that make great actors. His untiring faithfulness and unprecedented fruitfulness as an evangelist using these gifts to express those instincts are well known, and in this regard he is beyond anyone's power to imitate. His closest friends stood in awe of his seemingly endless energy in ministry—an eighty-hour working week for over thirty years, with no regular time off, preaching most days, sometimes three times a day, ministering informally in people's homes between and after services, starting early, finishing late and going on and on till finally his health broke and he died at fifty-five of what he thought was asthma but more likely was angina. Less well-known, however, is that Whitefield, like his older contemporaries John Wesley and Jonathan Edwards, was always clear that personal holiness—the Christ-like blend of love, lowliness and radical purity—is the supreme goal for every child of God, starting with himself; and that therefore, as a young Christian, again like Wesley and Edwards, he drew up for himself a private rule of life, focused in a series of questions for daily self-examination. All three were known by their intimates as genuinely humble men, despite their transcendent gifts and, in Wesley's case, temperamental bossiness; and surely the secret of that humility (meaning freedom from the swelled head that their achievements might otherwise have induced) was the realism about their continued shortcomings that their regular self-scrutiny induced. Here, now, are the questions that Whitefield put to himself at each day's end. Have I:

1. Been fervent in prayer?
2. Used stated hours of prayer? [i.e., turned to prayer at pre-planned times]
3. Used ejaculatory prayer each hour?
4. After or before every deliberate conversation or action, considered how it might tend to God's glory?
5. After any pleasure, immediately given thanks?
6. Planned business for the day?
7. Been simple and recollected [i.e., God-centered and self-controlled] in everything?
8. Been zealous in undertaking and active in doing what good I could?
9. Been meek, cheerful, affable in everything I said or did?
10. Been proud, vain, unchaste, enviable [i.e., envious] of others?
11. [Been] recollected in eating and drinking? Thankful? Temperate in sleep?
12. Taken time for giving thanks...?
13. Been diligent in studies?
14. Thought or spoken unkindly of anyone?
15. Confessed all sins?[5]

I am, I admit, something of a Whitefield groupie, and not just because I was educated at the school of which he remains the most distinguished alumnus (the Crypt School Gloucester[6]). As a minister of the gospel, I find constant devotional inspiration in Whitefield, not so much in any particular thing that he said or did as in what he was—an honest man who, in what he might have called a recollected way, was warm-heartedly abandoned to Christ, his cause, his praise and his glory, and he was totally free from self-seeking as a motive for action. Like C.H. Spurgeon, Martyn Lloyd-Jones and many others, I find the man himself, with his single-mindedness, initiative, friendliness, boldness, good humour and apostolic zeal endlessly challenging and strengthening. He has been called one of the most repulsive characters in the history of the Western world, but I for one find him supremely attractive. His life story, especially as told by sober Luke Tyerman, lively John Pollock and painstaking Arnold Dallimore, together with his journals, letters, sermons and occasional small writings, have been renewing and sharpening my sense of God for decades, even while the man himself seems to me greater than anything he said, wrote, or has had written about him thus far. Make Whitefield one of your traveling companions in ministry—indeed, in life—and I am confident you will get great benefit from his company, just as I have done.

Gruff and reserved, but Whitefield-like in his warm-heartedness, Christ-centeredness and, to use the old phrase, passion for souls, John Charles Ryle (1816–1900) is the fourth friend I introduce here. He was an early Victorian evangelical who from the 1850s on was Britain's premier tract-writer and who served with distinction from 1880 to the year of his death as the Church of England's first Bishop of Liverpool. Son of a banker and nurtured in luxury for leadership, with a political career set before him, Ryle became a clergyman when the bank broke, the family was reduced overnight to penury and he had to find wage-earning employment at short notice. As an evangelical minister, however, with a fine mind and flow of speech and a great deal of energy, he was dynamic from the start. Soaking himself in the works of Reformers and Puritans, he was soon a magisterial exponent of applied gospel truth (see, for proof of this, *Holiness, Practical Religion, Old Paths, The Upper Room* and *Warnings to the Churches,* plus his *Expository Thoughts* on each of the four Gospels) and with that he became an equally magisterial presenter of major figures in the evangelical past (see, for this, *Five English Reformers* and *Christian Leaders of the Eighteenth Century*). He did not write specifically for clergy—he was, in fact, a scholarly popularizer with a lay audience always in view—but his theological clarity, didactic brilliance and steam-hammer rhetoric combined with the blunt, searching quality of his down-to-earth applications make his material a powerful pick-me-up devotionally for ministers as much as for anyone else. Following is a sample of what I mean.

...The true secret of doing great things for God is, to have great faith.

I believe that we are all apt to err on this point. We think too much, and talk too much, about graces and gifts and attainments and do not sufficiently remember that faith is the root and mother of them all. In walking with God, a man will go just as far as he believes, and no further. His life will always be proportioned to his faith. His peace, his patience, his courage, his zeal, his works—all will be according to his faith.

You read the lives of eminent Christians, of such men as Wesley or Whitefield or Venn or Martyn or Bickersteth or Simeon or McCheyne. And you are disposed to say, "What wonderful gifts and graces these men had!" I answer, you should rather give honour...to their faith. Depend on it, faith was the mainspring in the character of each and all.

I can fancy someone saying, "They were so prayerful; that made them what they were." I answer, why did they pray much? Simply because they had much faith. What is prayer, but faith speaking to God?

Another perhaps will say, "They were so diligent and laborious; that accounts for their success." I answer, why were they so diligent? Simply because they had faith. What is Christian diligence, but faith at work?

...And another will cry, "it was their holiness and spirituality; that gave them their weight." For the last time I answer, what made them holy? Nothing but a living realizing spirit of faith. What is holiness, but faith visible and faith incarnate?

Now does any reader of this paper desire to grow in grace, and in the knowledge of our Lord Jesus Christ?...I dare be sure that every believer will reply, "Yes! Yes!" ...Then take the advice I give you this day: go and cry to the Lord Jesus Christ, as the disciples did, "Lord, increase our faith."[7]

On Christian basics across the board, Ryle has unique power to invigorate—and what pastor or lay leader practicing self-care should not or will not welcome that? Few match him at keeping us spiritually honest and on our toes at the same time. And his probes dig deeper and his visions of life in Christ shine brighter every time you reread him. Here, then, is gospel-soaked devotion that neither dates nor palls.

My fifth friend (no, I never met him, though we were in Oxford at the same time) is C. S. Lewis, the theologically literate High Churchman who died in 1963. As a devotional resource for clergy he may seem a strange choice, for he was an Oxford oddity, boyish and quixotic in his very mature adulthood and eccentric in a whole series of ways, and his Christian writings are either for complicated and wayward layfolk like himself or for children who have not yet got beyond being childlike. But his own past journeying into and out of unbelief gave him deep insight into temptation, conversion, repentance, faith, love, hope and evil, and his unique blend of logic and imagination makes this insight profoundly vivid and luminous in whatever form he presents it. For pastors, whose very familiarity with holy things constantly betrays them into superficiality of grasp, triteness of utterance and dryness of heart, Lewis's legacy is a wellspring of refreshing excitement. Two extracts will, I think, show what I mean.

The first comes from Lewis's quiet but awesomely wise last book, *Letters to Malcolm: Chiefly on Prayer.* It deals with what the admonition to place oneself in the presence of God when one prays really involves. Lewis speaks first of the personal "stage-set" for living that each one builds by selective intelligence, filtering impacts from outside through the meshes of social training and felt needs. Then he says:

> ...what I call "myself" (for all practical, everyday purposes) is also a dramatic construction; memories, glimpses in the shaving-glass, and snatches of the very fallible activity called "introspection", are the principal ingredients. Normally I call this construction "me," and the stage set "the real world."
>
> Now the moment of prayer is for me—or involves for me as its condition—the awareness, the reawakened awareness, that

this "real world" and "real self" are very far from being rock-bottom realities. I cannot, in the flesh, leave the stage, either to go behind the scenes or to take my seat in the pit; but I can remember that these regions exist…The dramatic person could not tread the stage unless he concealed a real person…And in prayer this real I struggles to speak, for once, from his real being, and to address, for once, not the other actors, but—what shall I call Him? The Author, for he invented us all? The Producer, for He controls all? Or the Audience, for He watches, and will judge, the performance? …The prayer preceding all prayers is, "May it be the real I who speaks. May it be the real Thou that I speak to." …Only God Himself can let the bucket down to the depths in us.[8]

Pastors particularly need to have these things consciously in mind when they turn to personal prayer, for we carry around with us a public identity that shields us from seeming to be what we truly are. Sin in our spiritual system guarantees this effect. Left to ourselves, we remain largely hidden from ourselves, and we need God to unmask us to ourselves. Realizing this is the entry-point for the divine action that ministers to this need of ours; the very awareness of our situation as self-ignorant creatures in God's presence allows, as Lewis writes, "at every moment, a possible theophany. Here is the holy ground; the Bush is burning now."[9] Vital prayer starts here, with real integrity growing as again and again we are searched by our God. *Letters to Malcolm* is the one book on praying that I reread: to all who have not yet encountered it (and it is not very well known) I strongly recommend it.

The second sample is the close of *The Last Battle*, the seventh Narnia story, where Lewis's power to communicate a sense of the glory of the biblical heaven—a sense that pastors above all, with our life-and-death involvements, need to have—finds perhaps its most potent and poignant expression. Writing for children aged eight to eleven—though happy for adults to read about Narnia, as it were, over the children's shoulders—and conceiving Aslan the lion as a true myth of Jesus Christ, Lewis pens the following:

> Then Aslan turned to them [the group of children] and said: "You do not yet look as happy as I mean you to be."
>
> Lucy said, "We're so afraid of being sent away, Aslan…"
>
> "No fear of that," said Aslan. "Have you not guessed?"
>
> Their hearts leaped and a wild hope rose within them.
>
> "There *was* a railway accident," said Aslan softly. "…all of you are—as you used to call it in the Shadowlands—dead. The term is over: the holidays have begun. The dream is ended: this is the morning."
>
> And as He spoke He no longer looked to them like a lion; but the things that began to happen after that were so great and beautiful that I cannot write them…But for them it was only the beginning of the real story. All their life in this world and all their adventures in Narnia had only been the cover and title page: now at last they were beginning Chapter One of the Great Story which no one on earth has read: which goes on for ever: in which every chapter is better than the one before.[10]

Small wonder, to any who read this, that George Sayer's stepdaughter, "after she had read all the Narnia stories, cried bitterly, saying, 'I don't want to go on living in this world. I want to live in Narnia with Aslan.'" Small wonder that Sayer, having recorded this, should add: "Darling, one day you will."[11] Small wonder that readers of Lewis the world over, clerical and lay alike, bless God for the devotional lift he brings them in terms of both a deeper acquaintance with their God and themselves and a sharper longing for what, after all, is their own true home. I hope that, with me, you who read this will join their number.

A final word, now, to my fellow-clergy. We affirm our need of renewal, and rightly so. Qualitative newness in our discipleship and service is something we all need to seek. But note that flanking NEW in the middle of *renewal* are the letters RE in front and AL behind, making REAL when put together. Here, I think, is not just whimsy, but wisdom. The quest for renewal must ever be a quest to be real before God, recognizing that in terms of what Christian life and ministry are supposed to be, we are not quite real yet. Centre self-care here, as my five friends will help us do, and I am confident that lives will be enriched and ministries transformed.

ENDNOTES

1. William Perkins, *A Graine of Musterd-seede,* quoted from J.I. Packer, *An Anglican to Remember* (London: Sr. Antholin's Lecture, 1996), 13–16. The full text is in Ian Breward, ed., *The Work of William Perkins* (Abingdon, UK: Sutton Courtenay Press, 1969), 404–410 and in Perkins' *Workes I* (1616), 642–44.

2. Cited from Richard Baxter, *The Reformed Pastor,* ed. William Brown, with an introduction by J.I. Packer (Edinburgh: Banner of Truth, 1974), 16.

3. Ibid., 61–62.

4. Ibid., 68–70.

5. Cited from Donald S. Whitney, *Spiritual Disciplines for the Christian Life* (Colorado Springs: NavPress, 1991), 204–205.

6. Not Bristol, as in Harry Stout, *The Divine Dramatist* (Grand Rapids: Eerdmans, 1991), 2, 5;

7. J. C. Ryle, *Holiness* (Moscow, Idaho: Charles Nolan, 2001), 176–77.

8. C. S. Lewis, *Letters to Malcolm: Chiefly on Prayer* (London: Geoffrey Bles, 1964), 108–109.

9. Ibid., 109.

10. C. S. Lewis, *The Last Battle* (Harmondsworth: Penguin [Puffin], 1964), 165.

11. George Sayer, *Jack: A Life of C.S. Lewis,* 2d ed. (Wheaton: Crossway, 1994), 319.

PART TWO: SERMONS

CHAPTER 7

THE FOOLISHNESS OF PREACHING

Harry S. D. Robinson

In the first three chapters of the first epistle of Paul to the Corinthians, Paul was wiser than he knew when he called preaching "foolishness." As Claude Laydu marvels in George Bernanos' novel *The Diary of a Country Priest,* "Every Sunday in France, ten thousand sermons are preached, and still there is faith," I similarly marvel that in Canada every Sunday in 1,800 Anglican parishes, the parish priest climbs into the exalted position in the pulpit and solemnly holds forth for ten minutes to half an hour, and still there is faith. The chronic tragedy of many parishes is that the organist can't hear himself or herself play, and the preacher can't hear himself or herself preach. A really successful sermon may leave the preacher with a foreboding sense of utter failure; a really poor sermon may leave the preacher with a deceptive sense of swelling accomplishment. If sermons were like furnaces, one would keep you warm for about twenty years—but even the best sermon only seems to warm the congregation for an hour or two before the damp chill sets in and the content is forgotten.

Miraculously many people come back week after week—though for some, they return not because they have been helped by a sermon, but because they have forgotten it.

Within the context of the liturgy, even if a sermon fails, the liturgy will apply first aid to the listeners. If the congregations are properly scandalized by the sermon, the liturgy will only confirm the essentially scandalous nature of the gospel in eloquent and precise language, correcting any heresy in the sermon and affirming that the gospel is indeed a scandal. Liturgy is an enormous support to the preacher—who at the end of most sermons needs confession and absolution. After delivering a sermon, the preacher is typically emotionally drained, intellectually exhausted and without any trust in his or her own righteousness—which, of course, is the place where every preacher ought to be—and the place where the preacher should be leading the congregation.

But there is a tendency in the Anglican Church to retreat from the high office of preaching the Word and to become engrossed in ordering the liturgy with all the eloquence of language, the dignity of office, the pomp and circumstance, the relevant and irrelevant ritual and the deceiving whisper that insidiously tempts the priest to think, "Thank God I'm not like others—robbers, evil-doers and adulterers." Though every priest may suffer profound humiliation in the "foolish" act of preaching, it is a much healthier condition than the deceiving arrogance that can come from playing with the liturgy. I love G. K. Chesterton's description of the difference between adults and children: children spend hours in make-believe, but they know that it's make-believe; adults spend hours in make-believe, but they don't know that it isn't. One of the requirements of the priest and the preacher is that he or she becomes as a little child and knows the difference between make-believe and reality.

The term "foolishness" was the response to Paul's declared strategy in evangelizing the Corinthians, when he announced that he was "resolved to know nothing while I was with you except Jesus Christ and him crucified." Corinth was a great city of the Ancient Greek world, and Greek culture had an enormous influence on Western culture, but Paul is careful to point out that even in Corinth, the prevailing wisdom proved its inadequacy and had to be replaced by God's secret wisdom, which they did not—and could not—understand by themselves. The prevailing wisdom nevertheless remained loyal to itself in declaring that the message of the cross was foolishness.

The Greek culture was the first among many subsequent cultures (right up to our own day) to regard the message of the cross as foolishness. Immersed in Greek culture, St. Paul, in the particular, peculiar and extremely sophisticated culture of Corinth, maintained a defiant agenda: his determination was to know nothing save Jesus Christ and him crucified. The public response—based on the prevailing wisdom—was that what Paul was saying was contemptuous and blasphemous foolishness. As it was then, so it is now. Human religion is almost always made up of bits and pieces of the prevailing wisdom of the age, so the response to the gospel now is the same: that it is foolishness. Paul wrote Acts chapter eighteen on the basis of his agenda to know nothing save Jesus Christ and him crucified. To a congregation of devout, miracle-seeking Jews and wisdom-seeking Gentile worshipers, Paul reasoned, preached, testified, persuaded and taught—and the congregation became abusive in response, forced him to leave, brought him before the magistrate (to no avail) and subjected at least one of his hearers to mob violence. (That hearer was Sosthenes, who had been a ruler of the synagogue before he heard about Jesus, with whom Paul wrote his first letter to the Corinthian church.)

Paul's determination to know nothing save Jesus Christ and him crucified inevitably destroyed the wisdom of the wise, frustrated the intelligence of the intelligent and revealed that human strength, ingenuity and eloquence were not sufficient to realize our human longings and ambitions. Paul himself was a Jew for whom Jesus Christ crucified was an enormous stumbling block—and for a time, he was determined to remove it. The Jewish aspirations for a miracle, and the massive accumulation of Greek wisdom, convinced Paul that to worship a crucified Galilean was blasphemous foolishness until he personally encountered Jesus Christ crucified. So we, in our turn, find it extremely difficult—immersed as we are in our own very sophisticated culture—not to regard the exercise of preaching as foolishness and the prescribed content of the sermon as foolishness. We find ourselves very susceptible to feeling shame among the articulate and intelligent people of our time. Shame again seals our lips when we are among the wealthy and the influential, the elite of our liberal democracy: the scholars, philosophers and those responsible for the enormous achievements in science and technology of our age. There is the added embarrassment that our words—no matter how eloquently we might preach the wisdom from God's Word—ultimately seem powerless. We are required to preach from a position of weakness—and are humiliated even further when we discover that the wise, influential and noble seem deaf, while only the weak, lowly and despised seem able to hear and respond.

I recently heard a helpful illustration about a time when Dwight L. Moody was walking through the streets of Chicago, and a drunk came up, confronted him and spoke to him; a bright spark who was with him said, "Doctor Moody, is that one of your converts?" To which Dwight Moody replied, "Yes, cause he certainly isn't one of God's." God seems to have failed to the point of foolishness in trusting his message to the foolish, weak, contemptible and despised. It would be so much more congenial if we might be called in ministry to preach to people whose main problem is that they are having difficulty getting a camel through the eye of a needle.

Paul's experience of preaching in these circumstances seems to have been very stressful. His sermons (by his own description) were delivered in fear and trembling; they were inarticulate and without evident human wisdom. Preaching does seem to demand that you mount the pulpit filled with inappropriate confidence and that you dismount with a profound sense of appropriate humiliation. If Paul contends that at the heart of our preaching is Jesus Christ and him crucified, inevitably we must suffer personally the verdict of our world, which is that the gospel is foolishness.

Nevertheless, in our persistent foolishness as preachers of the Word, we demonstrate that the real foolishness belongs to those who make the accusation—not to those they accuse. In Paul's brilliant assessment of the prevailing wisdom of Corinth, he says, "It was a wisdom that could never lead to the knowledge of God." The wisdom of Corinth produced proud structures that would inevitably perish. Our innate ability to see, hear and imagine—that is to see with our eyes, hear with our ears and to imagine with our minds—does not relieve us of our utter dependence on the revelation that God makes in Jesus Christ alone and him crucified. Paul further asserts that the prevailing wisdom will be destroyed and the intelligence of the elite will be frustrated. The ultimate failure of the prevailing wisdom was that it crucified the Lord of Glory.

The hidden wisdom of God lies beyond the range of human eyes, ears or reason. We confront this hidden wisdom only in the person of Jesus Christ crucified—and this is the reality with which the church must confront our present age. This is particularly challenging since our age has enormously enhanced the eye's ability to see, the ear's ability to hear, and stands in awe of what the human mind can conceive. Many preachers seem to desire to express the gospel in terms that are acceptable to the prevailing wisdom of our age, but Paul insists that the prevailing wisdom will always find Jesus Christ crucified utterly incomprehensible and therefore foolish. The agenda of our preaching, therefore, must not be to give meaning to the gospel within the bounds of the prevailing wisdom by adapting the ancient wisdom of the Scriptures to the new wisdom of our own generation, but to argue, persuade, testify, preach and teach that in Jesus Christ and him crucified, the prevailing wisdom has failed and the secret wisdom of God is revealed. Our world desperately needs preachers of such foolishness.

CHAPTER 8

THE GOSPEL OPPORTUNITY AND OUR CRISIS

David Short

After this Jesus revealed himself again to the disciples by the Sea of Tiberias; and he revealed himself in this way. Simon Peter, Thomas called the Twin, Nathanael of Cana in Galilee, the sons of Zebedee, and two others of his disciples were together. Simon Peter said to them, "I am going fishing." They said to him, "We will go with you." They went out and got into the boat; but that night they caught nothing. Just as day was breaking, Jesus stood on the beach; yet the disciples did not know that it was Jesus. Jesus said to them, "Children, have you any fish?" They answered him, "No." He said to them, "Cast the net on the right side of the boat, and you will find some." So they cast it, and now they were not able to haul it in, for the quantity of fish. That disciple whom Jesus loved said to Peter, "It is the Lord!" When Simon Peter heard that it was the Lord, he put on his clothes, for he was stripped for work, and sprang into the sea. But the other disciples came in the boat, dragging the net full of fish, for they were not far from the land, but about a hundred yards off. When they got out on land, they saw a charcoal fire there, with fish lying on it, and bread. Jesus said to them, "Bring some of the fish that you have just caught." So Simon Peter went aboard and hauled the net ashore, full of large fish, 153 of them; and although there were so many, the net was not torn. Jesus said to them, "Come and have breakfast." Now none of the disciples dared ask him, "Who are you?" They knew it was the Lord. Jesus came and took the bread and gave it to them, and so with the fish. This was now the third time that Jesus was revealed to the disciples after he was raised from the dead. When they had finished breakfast, Jesus said to Simon Peter, "Simon, son of John, do you love me more than these?" He said to him, "Yes, Lord; you know that I love you." He said to him, "Feed my lambs." A second time he said to him, "Simon, son of John, do you love me?" He said to him, "Yes, Lord; you know that I love you." He said to him, "Tend my sheep." He said to him the third time, "Simon, son of John, do you love me?" Peter was grieved because he said to him the third time, "Do you love me?" And he said to him, "Lord, you know everything; you know that I love you." Jesus said to him, "Feed my sheep. Truly, truly, I say to you, when you were young, you girded yourself and walked where you would; but when you are old, you will stretch out your hands, and another will gird you and carry you where you do not wish to go." (This he said to show by what death he was to glorify God.) And after this he said to him, "Follow me." Peter turned and saw following them the disciple whom Jesus loved, who had lain close to his breast at the supper and had said, "Lord, who is it that is going to betray you?" When Peter saw him, he said to Jesus, "Lord, what about this man?" Jesus said to him, "If it is my will that he remain until I come, what is that to you? Follow me!" The saying spread abroad among the brethren that this disciple was not to die; yet Jesus did not say to him that he was not to die, but, "If it is my will that he remain until I come, what is that to you?" This is the disciple who is bearing witness to these things, and who has written these things; and we know that his testimony is true. But there are also many other things which Jesus did; were every one of them to be written, I suppose that the world itself could not contain the books that would be written. (John 21)

There is no doubt that the church is in crisis—a crisis that involves a loss of faith, a loss of confidence and a loss of precious church members. But I think many of us are convinced that the crisis is also a moment of great opportunity, and we are being driven back to the foundation, to the person of the risen Christ himself. All four Gospels record that Jesus was raised from the dead, and in each one of the Gospels, the resurrection begins an entirely new moment. It is a new moment for Jesus Christ himself, as all authority is given to him. It is a new moment for the world—for the new creation has begun, and this world is passing away. And it is a new moment for the disciples, as Jesus takes the opportunity, in each of the Gospels, to transfer his mission to his disciples.

In chapter 20 of John, this new moment is marked by a movement from sight to faith. The risen Jesus meets Mary and transforms her grief into joy. The risen Christ meets the disciples and transforms their fear into delight. The risen Jesus meets Thomas and transforms his unbelief into belief. And the question is: What does the new moment mean for us today?

As we come to chapter 21, the final chapter of John's Gospel, it seems like such an anti-climax. We move from the magnificence of the resurrection of Jesus to a fishing story. We move from the Gospel, which contains the seven "I am" sayings, the great signs, the resurrection of Jesus and the promise of the Spirit. We move from the eternal Word made flesh and the promise of eternal life onto the beach, and it seems so mundane. But I think that this is John's point. Chapter 21 opens with a double reference to Jesus revealing himself. Look at verse 1: "After these things Jesus revealed himself to the disciples by the sea of Tiberias. And he revealed himself in this way… " This is not just a resurrection appearance tacked on to the end of the Gospel because John or the committee could not decide where to put it. Jesus' purpose here is not so much to give his disciples proof of his bodily resurrection; his appearance now reveals the permanent relationship that is going to exist between the resurrected Christ and his struggling disciples.

That is why it is so important for us today. John finishes his Gospel pointing out what it is going to mean that Christ is risen, pointing to the on-going, permanent relationship with Christ, who has now ascended into heaven. John gives us two episodes that show us what this means.

The first I have called "Fishing with the Risen Jesus" (verses 1 to 14). In verse 3, seven of the disciples decide to go fishing. Peter announces that he is going to go, and they say, "We'll join in." And they toil all night without success. Any romance that had crept up on them about this fishing business while they were with Jesus is quickly decimated. It's a complete waste of time. And my guess is that they come to the point that many of us have come to, where you've been doing something over and over and over again like throwing out your line or your net into the dark, just hoping that something will happen, and you begin to wonder about your own sanity.

It's a great picture, I think, of the Anglican Church. So often in this Gospel Jesus allows his disciples to toil at something without success, because he wants to give them a greater gift that's part of what it means to belong to the risen Christ. So much of what we do seems useless. Part of what we are being taught here is that in the circumstances that appear to be unfruitful and impossible, even the crisis which seems to have no purpose, God is leading us to some kind of greater blessing. After all, if everything fell automatically into place for us, we would be more unbearable than we are now—and almost entirely unteachable. In verse 4 we are told that Jesus is on the beach, and they do not recognize him—not because Jesus is hiding, but because they are not looking for him. He calls out, "Have you caught anything?" And they say, "No." And he says, "Cast the net on the other side!" If you have been fishing all night and not caught anything you are willing to try just about anything, and so without any discussion they throw the net on the other side. And suddenly they have a new and different problem: now the fish fill the net. It is a lovely picture of Jesus' mastery and control. Again, it is told—as all the miracles are in John's Gospel—with such reserve. Here is the risen Jesus, interested in and caring about this utterly mundane fishing expedition, and even the fish obey him.

It is a wonderful story. You don't need to spiritualize it or allegorize it—the plain facts speak for themselves. Jesus is risen from the dead; he is ascending to God the Father. Why is he interested in the bad fishing venture of these seven men? We move from the sublime heights of chapter 20 and the resurrection into this fishing debacle. It is too much for all the commentators, and they don't get it. Many of them have taken chapter 21 and tried to throw it back somewhere else into the Gospel.

But the point is simply that anything that concerns us—whatever you and I struggle with—concerns Jesus. This is the permanent way of the risen Lord with us, and this is why John recognizes Jesus and whispers to Peter, "It is the Lord." John is not afraid in the resurrection stories to keep referring to the fact that he's faster than Peter! He was faster to the tomb. He was faster to believe. And now here in chapter 21, he's faster to perceive that it is Jesus. He is more sensitive to the hand of God, and he's not afraid to tell us. But while he is quicker to see, Peter is quicker to act. He dives into the water, leaving the other six to struggle back to the beach with the full net. When they get back to the beach, Jesus has set a barbeque, and he is cooking breakfast and invites them to join him. The point is that the risen Christ continues to do for his disciples what he did before he was crucified, when he washed their feet—now they come to the beach and he serves them, and it makes them distinctly uncomfortable. This is what it means to follow Jesus. Here is a picture of the ongoing and permanent relationship that we have with him. Jesus has not stopped being interested in the daily circumstances of our lives, and he continues to serve us.

The second episode I have called "Following the Risen Jesus" (verses 15 to 25). As soon as breakfast is finished, Jesus asks Peter the same question three times: "Simon, son of John, do you love me more than these?" It's a very moving episode. Peter is profoundly aware that he denied Jesus three times. He is overwhelmed with a sense of his own failure: "How can I possibly serve Jesus? I am so shallow. I am so weak. I cannot possibly be of any use to Jesus Christ." Peter has dabbled in ministry and he has found himself constitutionally and personally unfit. But you know what? It doesn't seem to worry Jesus too much. Jesus' purpose in asking Peter this question three times is not to publicly humiliate him but to restore him. Three times Peter denied Jesus before his enemies; now in the presence of his friends, Jesus gives Peter the opportunity to affirm his love for Jesus three times. Jesus will not give up on Peter.

Don't you find it interesting that the key to developing Peter's leadership and potential in ministry is the realization of his forgiveness? You can't serve Christ or teach and lead others without first understanding the depth of your own forgiveness. Jesus probes Peter with the painful question, "Do you love me more than these?" because that's what Peter had boasted before the crucifixion: "They may all fall away, but I will never fall away. I will die before I deny you." And Peter says to Jesus, "Despite my bitter failure, the failure that you predicted, you know that I love you." And a second time, and then a third time, Jesus says, "Simon, son of John, do you love me?"

Jesus is not so interested in questions of performance or achievement or giftedness. He does not measure you and me by our failures or by what other people think of us. What Jesus asks us is, "Do you love me?" You may very well feel like Peter does. You may feel utterly and totally inadequate to serve him. You may have even let Jesus down badly—though perhaps not as publicly as Peter—and you feel crushed by an overwhelming sense of your own failure. "How could Jesus ever trust me?" you might wonder. But Jesus comes to us with forgiveness in his hands, and he says, "Do you love me?" His desire is not to humiliate us but to restore us to himself, to give us the forgiveness that he died to offer—and then to commission us for useful service.

It is only after Peter declared the truth of his love for Jesus that Jesus commissioned him. The commission is very simple: he says, "Feed my sheep." The primary requirement for feeding the flock is not remarkable abilities, great giftedness or that indefinable something that makes you a great leader. It is love for Jesus. This is the basic qualification for all Christian service and all ministry. While many of the other qualities are desirable, this is absolutely indispensable—without it, ministry becomes performance. Our ministry must be motivated by a love for Jesus, flowing out of gratitude for his forgiveness. This is where ministry begins, and it is particularly important for pastors—those who feed the flock.

In this last chapter of John's Gospel, Jesus defines the pastoral ministry in one way: "Feed my sheep," he says. This one verb—to feed, shepherd, tend the sheep—defines the ministry. Feeding the sheep means to move them into the pasture, to pastor them into the Word of God.

In verses 18 and 19, Jesus indicates that part of Peter's following him will mean martyrdom—as if martyrdom accompanies pastoral ministry. Peter thought he was very brave because he was willing to kill others for Jesus, but Jesus says the reverse is going to be true—his courage will be seen as he lays down his life for others. Jesus says, "Follow me." Then Peter asks about John's future—as if he doesn't want John to miss out on the great blessing of martyrdom! Jesus' gentle answer to Peter is, "Mind your own business. Follow me." Discipleship does not involve speculation, where you compare yourself to the discipleship of others. Your one responsibility is to follow Jesus, wherever that may lead.

Jesus' resurrection means that the risen and ascended Christ continues to serve us now, and the risen and ascended Christ calls on us to serve him. His service and our service are bound together by a four-fold chain that runs through chapter 21. The first element in the chain is *revelation:* the risen Christ continues to reveal himself to us in the mundane and ordinary things of life, in the places of frustration and unfruitfulness, where we are bewildered and baffled.

The second element in the chain is *restoration,* for Jesus not only reveals himself to us, but he asks us questions and probes our spirits in order to restore fellowship with him. The third element in the chain is *love*—our love for him, which rests on his love for us. "Do you love me?" he asks. And the reply he seeks is, "Lord, I do. You know I do." The fourth element in the chain is *service,* for if we love him, we will serve others. These four elements are bound together: revelation leads to restoration; restoration leads to love; love leads to service. Christ serves us by revelation and restoration; we serve him through love and ministry.

If you are thinking about pastoral ministry, you need to feed Christ's sheep by teaching God's Word to others—in small groups, youth groups, Sunday school. Ordination is not the beginning of ministry, it is the recognition of the reality of ministry. But feeding sheep is difficult. Speaking of John chapter 21, Calvin said,

> The office of feeding is in itself laborious and troublesome, since nothing is more difficult than to keep men under the yoke of God, among whom there are many who are weak, others who are dull and sluggish, and others who are slow and unteachable. Satan now brings forward as many causes of offence as he can, that he may destroy or weaken the courage of all good pastors. In addition to this, we may take into account the ingratitude, and other causes of disgust.

I would add that there is also the deep sense of our own inadequacy. Calvin goes on, "No one will steadily persevere in the discharge of this office unless the love of Christ shall reign in their heart in such manner that, forgetful of themself, and devoting themself entirely to Christ, they overcome every obstacle."

Jesus finishes this wonderful chapter with a double command: "Follow me...Follow me." Both times the command is in the present tense. Keep following me today—not next week, but now. "If you're out of the way, come back and follow me," he says. "If you're discouraged and feel isolated and alone, follow me." "If you feel you cannot do it, follow me."

PART THREE:
SEMINARS

CHAPTER 9

THE CHALLENGES OF RURAL MINISTRY[1]

Thomas O. Morgan

I think one of the greatest miracles of the New Testament, aside from the Resurrection, is Jesus' calling of the twelve disciples—including the "sons of thunder"—and the fact that he kept them together for three years. Any who have ever been in team ministry know the dynamics of even two people working together. In team ministry, only when you get the relationships worked out can you get on with the work. How did Jesus manage to get a team ministry of twelve working together effectively? Jesus' team only broke down when it looked like one of them was going to be killed. I do not think it is our job to try and analyze what happened to Judas, but the team held together as far as we can see, even though there was competition and "Who's going to sit at your right hand?" and "Who's going to sit at your left?" and the one who leaned on the breast of Jesus and the

---

1. Editor's note: This is the transcription of an informal address delivered at the conference.

one who declared, "Though everyone else forsake you, I won't!" (If you were a member of the team, what would that make you feel like? What do you think the others heard Peter saying about them in this remark?)

When you go into rural ministry, and you come to a little parish where you see only twelve people in the congregation, and you realize that this is what has been given to you, how do you make the most of that? Let's say that, like Jesus, you are on a cycle—a three-year term. How do you get away from the depressing thought that if you do not turn that twelve into twenty, you have failed? You can dream wonderful dreams, but if you go into a small town of 150 people with five churches, then you are not very likely to have 200 people coming to church every Sunday at the end of your ministry.

You will also have to deal with knowing that most of the money that parishioners give will go towards your salary. I found that really hard. Of course, I think giving joyfully is a part of our being Christians, yet it was not easy for me to know that so much of the energy of the parish went towards my pay. It did not seem to me like a gift to be so totally, transparently dependent on everyone. I wished that the money would come from somewhere else so that I would not have to be so visibly, viscerally dependant on that little group. At every annual meeting they would agonize over whether they could keep the church going for another year. But I learned that dependence is really what relationship is all about. That is what kept Jesus' little group of twelve together for so long; there was a kind of interdependence that actually worked.

Let us pretend that a person whose life has been essentially urban (someone from Calgary or Edmonton, so not big-time urban, but essentially urban) comes to a small town and suddenly finds that he or she is on a collision course with a person whose personality defects are similar to his or her own (i.e., both have a need for control). What should he or she do? Assert his or her place, and therefore depose someone who has been a part of "the twelve" for who knows how many years? In a rural ecology, if you are down the river, you dry up the swamp. You send away the birds, or you kill the coyotes or the deer that come in and eat your crops. In the little interrelated ecology of a congregation, people have spent years working out a coping mechanism—how to cope with the bossy one, how to live with the eccentric. If you come in and pull one of those people out, see what happens to the whole group! I'll go so far as to say they will never forgive you. They do not know how to create a new economy of relationships when you, who come in for a short time, demand that their relationships change. When it's over you will be gone, and they will never be able to revert to what they had known for years. Jesus knew how to receive twelve—and to receive them as a gift. When you come out of college (I'll speak for myself) your agenda is church growth, development, creating committees, setting up programs, creating community, finding a way to help people get to know each other—like wearing name tags to church. I don't want to poke at these; I think they are perfectly legitimate. But you can imagine what happens when you go in with an agenda to help these people get to know each other, and they have been living in a delicate ecological relationship for many years, knowing more than they should about each other anyway.

A friend of mine went to a small parish in Saskatchewan and just found it impossible. She was single, and on her day off she would get in the car and go somewhere. As soon as she was back somebody would ring her.

"I see you're home, where'd you go?"

"Well, I had my day off."

"Oh, did you go to Saskatoon?"

"Well, no."

"Oh, did you go down to Regina?"

"Well, actually, I went to such-and-such a place."

"Oh? What did you do there?"

"Well, I browsed around the shops."

"Did you buy anything? How much did you pay for it?"

And she was beside herself. But when she broke her leg, everybody knew about that, too, and they came to the door with cakes and casseroles until she couldn't believe it.

When I was living in Prince Albert, a big city of about 20,000, a Native woman said to me, "You white people have oneness."

I thought, "That's nice."

But then she continued, "You have one house here, you have one house here, and you have one house here."

In the rural community, there is oneness in a very different sense. Everyone does know everything, and it's okay. Of course there are some things you do not talk about—at least not to the people involved!

In a stewardship campaign, one of the things people have to do is go to their neighbors, preferably those they don't know too well or have a certain detachment from. It is almost impossible to get rural people to do this. It is like asking them to go and visit an uncle and hit him up for money. First of all, everyone knows how much money everyone else has, and how much money they are already giving. I knew a man who was the parish treasurer for many years, and at the end of the year he would send out a receipt to everyone on the list. If they hadn't given anything he would send them a receipt for nothing!

We have found the Alpha program very useful for engaging people who have never talked before. One of the reasons I think it works is that everyone in the room really gets to talk to each other, obliquely at first, but they end up actually talking very directly and personally. I think this is able to happen, in part, because Nicky Gumbel is not present, but he says things in the tapes that everyone in the room can react to—and they don't have to worry about offending him, because he is not there. This creates a kind of safety net. The program also asks the basic questions, such as, "Who is Jesus?" and "What is my relationship to Christ?" I think people have been longing to answer these questions for years, and whether it is intentional or unintentional, the program provides a safe way of discussing them, without having to feel that the priest is looking you in the eye and asking you to say something you haven't said for years. I have seen people in their eighties, who have only prayed alone before, begin praying in their Alpha group—a huge step for them. This program establishes a sense of a community, which is safe and respectful, in which you can ask any question or make any observation and you'll not be under judgement. I think that the twelve disciples survived together in rural communities by establishing such an environment.

I am not sure why it is so hard to get people into rural ministry. Some people in rural ministry, who are on their first appointment, feel that it is the first step on the ladder and that sooner or later they will "graduate." So it is important for you to think about whether you feel a long-term commitment to rural ministry. Can you see yourself there in the foreseeable future? I am not in rural ministry anymore, so it is not a question with a barb to it. But I think it is important for you to consider whether or not you feel that you can do something immensely significant for the kingdom of God with twelve people, twenty-five people—maybe even forty (not all rural congregations are tiny).

Jesus had three years with his twelve people—in three years at a church, you are just establishing relationships. But one of the amazing things about Jesus is that he established enormously close relationships very quickly. (Yet at other times he seems to feel, I've been this long with you and you *still* don't know? You *still* don't understand me?) I usually ask people to commit to a church for five years if they can, understanding that if after two years they just know it is not working and they have to reassess, then that is what must happen.

If you are going to have a successful ministry, you must first secure the centre; you must have a relationship with the core community. I think this is true for the city as well as the country. It may be easier in the country—or it may be more difficult, because the options are fewer. But I believe that if you do not secure the trust of the centre of the church community within your first two years, then it is very unlikely that you will get anywhere. If a priest is to mobilize people, he or she must have people who share the vision. Find the core and see if you can fall in love with each other, with all your eccentricities. In our diocese there are only two people in the Synod office, but I don't think I could survive without that group. There is transparency, honesty and a sense that we can just talk—I don't mean spill our guts, but that we can say whatever we want to, and there is a trust relationship.

My family once came into a very difficult parish experience where my predecessor had not secured the trust at the centre of the community. The wardens of that parish said, "We're not sure he trusts us! He doesn't give us anything to do—he's holding onto it all himself." I do not think any of that was intentional on the part of the priest, that it was a power trip. As far as I can see, he was a very fine priest, but there was always a sense in which he was standing on the edge, looking in. Rural ministry differs from urban ministry in that you do not have many options—so you must establish that trusting relationship with the few at the centre of the community. Even within Jesus' group of twelve there were the trusted three, who went up to the mount of transfiguration to see what nobody else did.

Roy Oswald says that first you are supposed to be the lover: you learn the history and fall in love with it; you get to know the people, and you learn to love them; you establish trust. Jesus said, "Do you love me?" and Peter winced, I think, because he couldn't quite bring the words back. He came as close as he could to saying, "I love you," and the wonderful thing is that Jesus said, "I trust you. Here's a job I'm going to give you: feed my sheep." He couldn't have been more trusting than to put the care of his own people into Peter's hands. A second time he asks, "Do you love me?" and Peter is still feeling badly, and Jesus says, "I trust you. Here's a job for you." The third time Peter says, "Why are you doing this to me?" Jesus replies (in my words), "I want you to know that I trust you. I'll take what you've got and give you the most important job there is: feed my sheep; tend my flock; look after them."

It was the evangelical world that challenged me to give my life to Christ. It was the evangelical world that called me to read the Scriptures and listen for the voice of God. It was also the evangelical world that taught me not to trust anybody but evangelicals. There is so much work to do—let's get at the work together. Let's feed the flock of Christ. Let's proclaim the evangel as best we can. Let's become a serving community and let the world know that there is life and hope.

What do you need for rural ministry? I think you need a huge generosity of spirit to imagine that God can use the kind of people you never dreamed you would have to work with. You must somehow be able to open up for them the Christ in you, and when they have seen that spark, you must fan it to life. I went to Tyndale Hall in the 1960s, when the evangelicals were on the fringe of the British church, and—for a very good reason, I think—they behaved like they were on the fringe. They attacked everything in the church they could see. Their mission was to save the church. And it was my mission, too: to save the church, to bring it back to its roots, and to call it to faithfulness.

I still believe my mission as a Bishop is to call the church to its centre and to embrace Christ at the centre, but somewhere along the way I have also fallen in love with the Anglican Church. If I were to interview you for a job in the parish, and if I were to ask you (and this would be quite deliberate) as the first question, "Tell me what you love most about the Anglican Church of Canada," would your mouth be left hanging open? It is very easy to put the question differently, to say, "What do you believe are the problems that need to addressed in the Anglican Church of Canada?" I believe that there is a profound law about ministry: "According to your faith be it done unto you." What you really believe, deep down within, you cannot disguise. If you believe that this church can nurture and bring to birth a new life, it will happen; but if in your heart you do not believe that this old church has actually got it, then don't try.

I remember preaching in Shelburg one time. I was trying to preach the gospel, the good news. Afterwards, one of the members of the congregation (who I never thought was at the heart of anything) came up to me and said, "Tom, whatever was wrong this morning?" He meant, "What was wrong with you, because you just left me in the pits!" I realized that no matter how much I tried to take the text and to preach life, I had preached out of my heart, which did not believe the message—and this came through. If you are in rural ministry and you wish you were somewhere else, then for goodness sake, go somewhere else! If you think these are dumb, ignorant farmers, you will never disguise it. What you really believe actually comes through. If you love people, even though they make you mad, they will make exceptions. They will allow you to blow sometimes.

I was with Aboriginal people for about nineteen years. If you tell Aboriginal people you love them, they respond, "Why do you need to tell me?" But people would come out and preach and tell the Aboriginals how much they loved them—people who had never been on the reserve before. They had no right to say they loved them; they did not even know them. The point is that what you really believe will find you out. I think our culture has taught Aboriginal people that they are marginal, that they are unimportant, and it is very difficult for them to believe otherwise. Similarly, rural people may wonder if you really like them and if you really want to be with their church, especially if nobody has ever stayed in the past. To convey to rural people, "You are important, and in terms of the circle of God's people, we stand shoulder to shoulder," you must live that out in a way that they can believe.

When you enter rural ministry you are immersing yourself in a culture that has its own life, a whole history. When I was in Newfoundland at the Synod, we were singing "Will Your Anchor Hold?" I was sitting next to a fisherman who had just been out—his hands were all cracked from the salt—and he told me that every time he went out in the boat, his wife would leave the light on in the window and then pray that God would bring him safely home. "Will your anchor hold in the storms of life" suddenly became an important metaphor. I had sung that hymn on the prairies, for goodness sake, and had loved it, but all of a sudden it took on new life. I went back to Saskatchewan searching for a Saskatchewan metaphor. I think it is "Lift up your eyes to the fields, and look, they're ripe for the harvest." Everyone in Saskatchewan knows about that. I remember standing on the doorstep of our house at the end of August. My father had just the day before been out to the hundred acres north to look at the crop, and you could see his heart swell with pride. And then we watched the thunderstorms come up and the hailstorm come through and wipe it out. There is a real urgency in Saskatchewan about the fields being ripe to the harvest, just as there is about having a secure anchor in the storm in Newfoundland.

I want to give you another example of a parish—one that is Anglican and United, a shared ministry, and it is what I would call "the popular church." It is where everybody is buried, where most people still come for baptism, where most marriages take place, but it has a very thin little group who actually come to worship. If that church began to answer, "No, you may not be baptized," and "No, you may not be married," and "No, you may not be buried here because, for whatever reason, you've sat lightly to the faith," it would seem to me somewhat similar to the Hebrews and the Jews saying, "No, you may not be circumcised. No, you may not belong to the covenant." There is an assumption in rural communities of *belonging,* which you can receive as a gift—and on which you can build. You must embrace the goodwill that is there, even if it is casual and light. Some people see that as a burden: "They only come to church to be married!" or "They only come to be baptized!" But do you want them to stay away?

Let's take those who come only for baptism, for example. Why is that a gift? Number one, they come. Number two—let's just assume the worst, that they know very little—they understand that the church has to do with God and their response to God. Number three, they think it is right. I happen to think so too. Go back to "According to your faith be it done unto you"—if you are glad to see them, they will know. If you are not, you will not fool them. I have learned to be glad, to say, "We'll start where we are." Baptism is about grace, not about obligation, so begin with the grace rather than the rules, the hoops they must jump through. I used to say to people, "When you bring your baby to be baptized, I am going to assist you—right up front. You can't throw the baby from the back! If you want to present your baby to God, you will have to present yourself to God, too, so let's talk about it." They laughed—they liked it! I would say, "Here's the gospel news: when you present yourself to God, God's going to say, 'Welcome, glad to see you. You've come. I'm glad. Let's get together.'" I see it as an opportunity to start where they are, to believe that there is a flame, maybe only a flickering flame, but a flame of goodness in their intentions. I cannot imagine somebody coming for evil reasons. Take it; receive that much as a gift, and go on with it. Some seed falls on shallow ground, springs up quickly and goes away; some takes root then gets attacked, eaten up and it goes away; but some takes root and produces one hundredfold. I do not think it is my job to say, "You get in, you don't." My job is to say, "You're approaching God; I want to go with you." And I have a deep sense that when any child is offered to God, angels are singing.

It seems to me the sense of belonging found in rural parishes is a gift, one that we can no longer assume in the city. When our adopted auntie came out to the farm, she went out on the front verandah and looked around, and she said to my mum and dad, "You must be so lonely." Mum said to her, "How many people do you know on your street?" Well, my auntie went down the list and named eight people. When Mum started naming the neighbors she went on and on, naming nearly a hundred. When Mum and Dad died, like so many other people in that community, you would not have believed how many people were there. The one thing that never occurred to them was to be lonely.

Rural ministry, then, is a gift—a gift to you and a gift to them. It requires love and perseverance. It requires finding and nurturing the centre. It still beckons people who will respond to Jesus' question and invitation to Peter: "Do you love me?...Feed my sheep."

CHAPTER 10

WHAT'S THE JOB AND WHAT ARE THE SKILLS REQUIRED?

Harold Percy

As Jesus was walking beside the Sea of Galilee he saw two brothers: Simon, called Peter, and his brother Andrew. They were casting a net into the lake, for they were fishermen. "Come follow me," Jesus said, "and I will make you fishers of men." And at once they left their nets and followed him. And going on from there he saw two other brothers, James the son of Zebedee and his brother John. They were in a boat with their father Zebedee, preparing their nets. Jesus called them, and immediately they left the boat and their father and followed him.

These words of Matthew record the beginning of the public ministry of Jesus. Down by the waterfront, watching these men fish, telling them to come and follow him, Jesus says he will teach them how to fish for people. Another passage at the very end of Matthew's gospel records the end of Jesus' ministry:

The eleven disciples went to Galilee to the mountain where Jesus had told them to go. When they saw him, they worshiped him, but some doubted. Then Jesus came to them and said, "All authority on heaven and on earth has been given to me. Therefore go and make disciples of all nations, baptizing them in the name of the Father and of the Son and of the Holy Spirit, and teaching them to obey everything I have commanded you. And surely I will be with you always, to the very end of the age." (Mt 28:16–20)

Here we have a passage from the very beginning of Jesus' public ministry and a passage from the very end of Jesus' public ministry, as recorded by Matthew. Herb Miller, a church consultant from Lubbock, Texas, has two books about the ministry of Jesus—one called *The Magnetic Church*, the other called *The Vital Congregation*. Of these passages he says: "Here's one at the beginning, one at the end. These passages represent what we could call the 'bookends' of Jesus' ministry. And they both have to do with evangelism." It is an interesting point to ponder, whether or not it was just coincidence or whether it was clearly thought out by Jesus that the first people he called were fishermen. Was it just a coincidence that he happened to be at the waterfront where the fisherman were gathering and doing their work, and he decided it was time to get this project underway? Or had a little bit of strategic planning gone into this? This moment is so rich in symbolism that it is hard for people who take it seriously to miss what he was about: "I'll choose some fisherman—that will surely give people a clue as to what I'm about! And as you come with me, I'm not really going to change who you are—you've already been fishing for fish, now I'm going to teach you how to fish for people." Then he takes the next months and years and he trains and equips his disciples, preparing them for the ministry of evangelism.

In the very last words we have recorded in Matthew's gospel, as Jesus is about to return to the Father, he gives his disciples their marching orders, saying, "Here's the program—you've got a whole world out there. You go and do what you've seen me do. You teach what I've taught you. And bring everybody in—make sure they all understand that the kingdom of God is open for business, and they're invited in." Herb Miller says, "if you read that seriously and sat down and thought about it, and let it kind of wash over your mind, you could be forgiven if you walked away from that with the impression that Jesus was interested in evangelism. You might just get a suspicion here that it was important to him." He continues by saying that if evangelism is important to Jesus, it should be important to us. As a matter of fact—and Herb Miller is a very careful writer, so this is a very radical statement—he says, "If you are one of those Christians, or if you are part of one of those congregations in our mainline churches today who say, 'I am not interested in evangelism,' or 'We're not interested in evangelism,' you better take another look at who it is you're following, because there's a good chance that it isn't Jesus."

People who follow Jesus are people who are interested in that ministry of fishing for people, telling them the good news of the kingdom and inviting them in. In the middle of Matthew's gospel, there's another passage:

> Jesus went through all the towns and villages teaching in the synagogues, preaching the good news of the kingdom, and heal-ing every disease and sickness. And when he saw the crowds he had compassion on them, because they were harassed and help-less like sheep without a shepherd. Then he said to his disciples, "The harvest is plentiful, but the workers are few. Ask the Lord of the harvest, therefore, to send out workers into his harvest field." (Matthew 9:35–38)

This passage—taken from the middle of Jesus' ministry—focuses on the same theme: the mandate of the church to reach the lost. A church that is going to be faithful is a church that thinks creatively and takes the initiative in developing ways to connect with the surrounding culture so that this good news can be shared—not a church that sits and waits for the culture to come to it. Some clergy that I meet in my work across this country communicate to me in various ways that they're getting impatient with their neighborhoods because "these people out here, they don't support the church!" These clergy are putting in a lot of effort, and they're frustrated, asking, "How can I get this community to support the church?"—as if the community is there to support the church!

The initiative and the responsibility for connecting with the culture rests with the church, because we are the ones that have been given the mandate to go and to share the good news. Reginald Bibby, a sociologist of religion at the University of Lethbridge said, "The last time I was down on the farm, it wasn't the job of the sheep to try and find the shepherd!" I think that's an important thing to keep in mind. We are facing challenging times in the church. We are not thriving the way we used to, and though there are all kinds of reasons why this is the case, I want to concentrate on one: the fact that the harvest has changed—because this is central for anyone considering a life of service and ordained ministry in the church.

Jesus loved to use metaphors about the harvest being ready and plentiful when he talked about how we can connect with the world and share the news of God's kingdom. But in our "postmodern," "post-literate," "post-denominational" generation and culture, where there is no longer "brand loyalty," the harvest has changed. Someone writing in the *Toronto Star* recently asked, "What's this about no denominational or brand loyalty? If someone asks me what shampoo I use, I always have the same answer: whatever they're selling for 99 cents!" That's the new brand loyalty!

In the book *How to Reach Secular People*, George Hunter from Asbury Seminary said,

> When the harvest changes, the harvesters have to change their method if they're going to be effective. So, if you are accustomed to harvesting corn and you've invested a lot of money in some pretty sophisticated corn pickers, and all of a sudden everything switches around and you're called to harvest grapes, those corn pickers aren't going to help you much. Chances are they're going to cause more trouble. You're going to have to learn some new skills if you're going to be able to harvest when the harvest changes.

This is the challenge we're facing in our mainline churches—and in the Anglican Church of Canada in particular.

Our church, in its congregational life, structures, mentality and temperament, has been set up to work in a culture that no longer exists. So our efforts are running into difficulties because we're trying to harvest wheat or grapes with corn pickers. Anglican congregations across Canada, because of their history, structure and self-understanding, were created for the Christendom era. These churches were built and planted in an age when it was safe to assume that you carried out your ministry among Christian people who shared a Christian worldview, who understood what you meant when you said "God" and who on Easter celebrated the resurrection. They didn't talk about butterflies coming out of cocoons—they celebrated the resurrection of Christ. And that worldview was reinforced at home, at school, in business and in government—it was just part of the air that we breathed.

This was so much the case that we talked—probably erroneously—about our Christian culture and actually went so far as to act and to speak as though "good Christian" and "good citizen" meant the same thing. When a congregation is set up to minister in this kind of a culture, the predominant style that shapes it is a pastoral ministry, which involves looking after the faithful and providing them with services of worship. Throughout the week pastors deal with issues that come up in the lives of those people that gather for worship—pastoral care, grief counseling, nurturing, rites of passage and those sorts of things. This ministry operates on a client/consumer kind of a mentality, where the people come to church as clients and consumers of the religious services run by somebody there who's paid to do that kind of ministry.

When this parish or congregation thinks about itself, it thinks about itself as a place that looks after the faithful as they go through their life seeking to live as Christian people. But the evidence could not be more compelling that this model is no longer appropriate. There used to be the expectation that if there was a new housing development, you could go in there and build an Anglican church, and all you had to do is put up a sign that said, "We're going to have a service at 10:00, everybody's welcome," and then you had to jump back because if you didn't, you'd get killed in the crush. Now you're more likely to die of loneliness! The theory of church growth that says, "We'll build a church and then wait for them to come," is a traditional model that cannot meet the challenge, because the mega-shifts in the culture mean that the assumptions behind it are no longer appropriate. As Loren Meade points out, in the Christendom era all the energy, all the dynamics of the whole culture contrived to move people towards the church. So in Christendom, if you were an upstanding citizen, a hard worker, raising your family, living an honest life, and you didn't go to church, somebody—maybe your neighbor, your boss or a family member—would ask you why. But in post-Christendom, all the energy of the culture moves you out of the church, and if you look like you're halfway intelligent and you still go to church, someone is going to ask you why. That reversal has taken place in about thirty-five years in this country. The difference in the culture is so marked that I agree with Bill Eason, who said that "the better that we do what was done in the past in terms of that chaplaincy/pastoral style of congregation, the better we do that, the quicker the church will die, the quicker that congregation will die, because it is just so inappropriate."

If we agree that the mandate of the church is to be able to connect with the culture and share the good news of God *in* and *as* Christ, and invite people into the life of Christ and the kingdom of God, then this means that in order to be faithful we have to change our methods. The evangelism strategy of the Anglican church—"Sooner or later, everyone of good taste will, in their own good time, become an Anglican"—is no longer adequate. Changing our methods does not imply a criticism of our past; it is simply an acknowledgment that the harvest has changed.

But what kind of congregation will it take to engage effectively with today's post-modern, post-Christendom, post-literate, superficially secular, pagan culture? How can we penetrate this culture with the gospel? How can we connect with the people who have been shaped by this culture, lead them to Christ and disciple them? In place of the former Christendom congregation—which sees itself as a center for pastoral care that exists for the good of its members who use its services—congregations must emerge that understand themselves as having a different purpose, a different inner urge and motivation than those that thrived in the Christendom era. These congregations are driven by the Great Commission and understand that Jesus' command to "go into all the world" and "to make disciples of all nations" carries at least as much weight as the command to "do this in remembrance of me," the one that we Anglicans really love. The effective congregation in this new harvest field is one that sees itself primarily as a centre for mission that is training and equipping workers for the harvest field—rather than as a centre for pastoral care. Such congregations do not measure congregational strength by how many people show up for worship on Sunday or how much money they give, but they are learning to measure congregational strength on the basis of how many members are sent out each week after worship trained, equipped and motivated to work in the harvest field, bearing witness to God's kingdom as ambassadors for Christ. For such a church, the key question when contemplating some kind of a change in its congregational life isn't, "Is this going to upset somebody here?"—which is the traditional kind of question—but rather, "Is this going to help us to reach more people from the outside?"

This sort of transformation does not involve tinkering on the edges of congregational life, but changing our congregational DNA, how we understand our identities and ministry. I believe that the primary job of congregational leadership is to nurture into existence a congregation that is thinking *out* instead of thinking *in;* and instead of being a centre for pastoral care, it is a centre for training and equipping workers for the harvest. What are the skills and strengths of a leader who can initiate the transformation of a typical, inwardly focused congregation into a centre for mission, capable of penetrating the surrounding culture and influencing it for Christ?

First, in most cases, I think these leaders need a solid academic foundation—particularly in biblical studies, church history and systematic and biblical theology. But though it is important that you get education, it is important because of the process—not because of the product. So second, these leaders need to be spiritually grounded and to have a vital devotional life—or, as Dallas Willard says, "living interactively with God." Without being deeply rooted in Christ and exercising the spiritual disciplines, you won't be much good to anybody for very long. But in these changing times, it is possible to have a solid academic foundation and to be spiritually grounded and to flounder in frustration as a congregational leader. So third, the congregational leader needs to develop the appropriate skill sets for transformational leadership in a congregational setting. There are three major categories of skills that are necessary for effective congregational leadership: developing basic leadership skills, making disciples and empowering people for ministry.

DEVELOPING BASIC LEADERSHIP SKILLS

First, the absolute prerequisite for good leadership in congregational life is the development of basic leadership skills, which begins with a strong sense of personal identity and calling. You need to know who you are and what your ministry is about. You have to be able to answer these basic questions: What do you want to do with your life? What do you want to God to do through you? When you get to the point where most of your years in ministry are behind you rather than in front of you, what do you want to be able to look back on with pride and a sense of accomplishment? Think deeply about these questions. This sense of calling and identity is the foundation on which to build other leadership skills.

Another component of basic leadership is that you need to have an unshakable conviction that the gospel of Jesus Christ is the good news of God—and the good news that this world needs to hear.

We have too many people leading our congregations right now who don't believe that the gospel can change people's lives, and their congregations are sad places because of that. You will also need to have the conviction that the gospel can change people's lives—that secular, selfish people can become followers of Jesus Christ.

There is an old proverb that says if you think you're leading and nobody's following, you're just taking a walk, so another key aspect of basic leadership is that leaders *lead*. They're not dictators or bullies; they don't manipulate. But a good congregational leader is able to bring a congregation together around a clear identity—teaching them what it means to be the people of God—and also around a clear purpose—teaching them what we're called to be and to do as followers of Christ and what God expects of the church. A good congregational leader will also take responsibility for casting a vision that motivates the people, energizing and inspiring them to seek to do great things with God for the community.

John Maxwell of Enjoy Life Ministries, who has devoted many years of his life to understanding leadership in congregational settings and works to equip clergy in leadership skills, says that there are five levels of leadership and influence, which he pictures as a set of steps.

The lowest level of leadership and influence in the congregation is the level of position, where people follow you because you're the rector, and the bishop put you there. At that level of leadership, people may come to church, but attendance is down, and the people who do come leave right after the service.

The second level of influence is the level of permission, where people follow you because they want to, and they say, "We really like him" or "We really like her." Lots of clergy strive to get to this place, and it certainly makes it easier if people like you, but at this level there's still not much happening except that maybe the people stand around and have a cup of coffee after church, and they talk to the priest and there's a nice kind of chemistry.

The third level of influence is the level of a production, where people say, "Wow, look at what this priest is doing." Church is getting better, more people are coming, more kids are in the Sunday School, young people are present, the giving is up. But it's still pretty much the priest's agenda.

The fourth level of influence is what John Maxwell calls a "people production," where people follow you because you're discipling them and equipping them for ministry. They say, "We go with this priest because I'm a better person," or "I'm a more mature Christian," or "I've got a great ministry here," or "My life is better because this person is working with me."

The fifth level of influence deals with personhood, but we don't need to worry about this level because it's reserved for people like Billy Graham, Desmond Tutu and Martin Luther King—people who have established such a reputation with their ministries that it's just an outpouring of who they are.

There are some important observations that should be made here. The first is that you have to go through each of the levels to get to the next level. Second, you can be on different levels with different people at different times. Most clergy get to level two—where people like you—but that's not sufficient to transform the DNA of a congregation. You start being effective when you get to level four, when the people are saying, "Wow, my life is being changed because of the ministry of the person here."

In my work with churches in this country, my overwhelming impression is that many—indeed, *most*—congregations don't have any vision of what they want to see happen in the future in their communities. They just keep doing the same thing for fifty-two weeks in a row in endless succession. You don't want to be a clergy person of whom it is said that you have ten years experience on paper, but the truth is that you only have one year's experience that you've repeated ten times. Clergy need to learn to lead their congregations through constructive change, which has to be rooted in a clear understanding of what it means to be the church—its identity and mandate. In theological terms this is called "ecclesiology." You also have to have an understanding of how the church can engage secular society—which is called "missiology."

When initiating change, congregational leaders need to communicate the larger vision for mission to the congregation. Otherwise, people may assume that the congregational leader is just changing things to suit his or her own preferences. If we are to be effective Anglican Church leaders, we must learn to use tradition as a rudder that enables us to follow God into the future rather than an anchor that imprisons us in our past. In Scripture, we encounter a God who invites us to look back at the past and says, "Just as I was faithful to your fathers in the past, when they came into that new situation, I'll be faithful with you in the future as I lead you into this one. But we're doing something new."

Leadership also requires good relational skills. If the people in your congregation get the sense that you love the "ministry," the "church" and your "career" before you love them, it is going to be hard to influence them.

MAKING DISCIPLES

The second essential element to good leadership in congregational life is the ability to make disciples. Congregational life is about transformation—not just transferring information. We need to help people seek to be changed by the Word of God as they learn to live lives in apprenticeship to Jesus Christ.

This work of discipleship has been tragically neglected in our mainline churches for several decades, and now we are reaping the sorry results of this neglect. Biblical illiteracy in congregations across Canada is scandalous. Some people have been in church for fifty years, paying money, sitting on committees, giving time and energy—but many don't know the difference between the New Testament and the Old Testament, and they're not familiar with the rhythms of Scripture. If you ask them to say grace at a church lunch, they respond by saying—or at least thinking—"What do you think we're paying you for? That's what you ought to do." People who are biblically illiterate and don't know how to pray aren't going to change anything—particularly themselves. Their vision won't go past the next fundraiser, and they'll fight about even that. Yet this is what they have been taught, so it is essential that transformation begin with the basic work of discipleship.

George Hunter says, "The problem with most Christian communicators in North America is that we start in the middle. We just assume way too much." I am not saying that we should reduce the gospel, but we should speak it simply and clearly from the beginning, assuming nothing. This is one of the reasons that Alpha is so popular—it starts at the beginning. As one saying goes, "If you shoot over people's heads, the only thing you prove is that you don't know how to shoot."

William Willamon has said, "Do not shrink the gospel in order to try and make it intelligible to modern people. Proclaim it in its fullness so that modern people can understand where their lives are unintelligible." If we speak in the name of God and people can't understand us, we sin against both God and those people. The work of the kingdom is done by disciples who are growing towards maturity, over time, out of the rough and raw material of selfish, secular people who have been infused with a vision of what it means to be followers of Jesus Christ.

EQUIPPING PEOPLE FOR MINISTRY

The third essential element to good leadership in congregational life is the ability to equip people for ministry. If you're going to transform your congregation and move it away from that client/consumer model, your goal must be to give your ministry away. If you try to hold onto it, it'll be like a pool of stagnant water. But if you keep giving it away, just letting it flow through, it'll always run clear and clean. You will know that you are really along the way when one day your people are so involved in ministry that they can look up and say, "Are you still here? Isn't there someplace you should be? Don't get in our way—we're doing ministry!"

There's an old proverb that says, "Of the very best leaders, it is said when the work is done and the goals have been reached the people say, 'We did it ourselves.'" And the leader just stands back, lights his cigar and says, "I love it when a good plan comes together." There's no limit to what can be accomplished in congregational life when the leader does not care who gets the credit—especially when the leader doesn't need to take the credit.

So as you consider ordained ministry in the Anglican Church, remember this call for transformational leadership and commit yourself to lifelong growth and development in these areas. Don't let anyone suck you into thinking about how you can save the church, because this will sap the life out of your soul. Instead, focus your attention on how you can reach the world. How can you connect this culture with the life-changing message of the gospel? If you stop thinking about how to save the church and train yourself to think about how to reach the world—or at least that little corner of the world that you're in—you might just find that you've helped to save the church, too, because as Jesus said, "Those who seek to save their life will lose it, but those who are willing to lose their life for my sake and for the gospel's will save it."

> May the God of peace, who through the blood of the eternal covenant brought back from the dead our Lord Jesus, that great Shepherd of the sheep, equip you with everything good for doing His will. And may he work in us what is pleasing to him, through Jesus Christ, to whom be glory forever and ever. Amen. (Hebrews 13:20)

CHAPTER 11

SHOULD I CONSIDER ORDINATION?

Reginald Hollis

Jesus said to the apostles in John 15:16, "You did not choose me, but I chose you and appointed you, that you should go and bear fruit." As Archbishop of Montreal, where I served for sixteen years, I was responsible for ordaining perhaps four or five people a year on average. I first got to know some of these people at youth camp, where they often discussed the possibility of being called to ordained ministry. Over the years, the most important thing that I wanted to know from all of them was whether they had a true sense of calling— if they felt that they had not chosen this work but rather had been chosen for it. They often had some worries about their abilities, but I wanted to know that this was something that really "bothered" them, something that they could not say "no" to, something that they felt they had to do.

There is no strict test for this knowledge, for being aware of the sense of call. Cosmo Gordon Lang, who was Archbishop of Canterbury from 1928 to 1942, and of York before that, was a law student at Oxford in the late nineteenth century. Once he rode his horse over to attend a friend's ordination. On his way, a voice came suddenly into his mind: "Why don't you be ordained?" The thought was utterly shocking to him. He first had to find a bishop and ask to be confirmed, because he had no prior connection with the church. Though it was a strange idea, it was one that persisted, and it brought him into a very fruitful ministry.

That did not happen to me; I had no sudden voice from heaven. In my early teenage years, I began to think that God had called me to the ministry. The idea was confirmed as I grew in years: doors opened and doors closed—I am a great believer in doors opening and closing to show us the way. I was supported in my local church as I became more and more involved—teaching Sunday school, reading Scripture at the invitation of the rector, leading Evensong and then preaching. The congregation encouraged me. It was important that I felt that sense of encouragement, because I also encountered some things that were not encouraging. My headmaster at school, for instance, was not encouraging. Every year there was a parents' night, and my father went. My father was not a church person at that point. The headmaster would say to him that I should not be going into the clergy, that I should be a lawyer. That appealed to my dad, because he knew there was money in being a lawyer and not in being a priest. He would come home and tell me so. One of the strangest things my headmaster said one year was, "He shouldn't be ordained—he doesn't have enough devil in him!" Well!

When I was nineteen years old, I went to the equivalent of ACPO (the Advisory Committee for Postulates for Ordination), the selection committee that in England is called CACTM (Central Advisory Council for the Training of the Ministry). I went for a week and was interviewed; afterwards I received a letter from them saying that they could not approve my training for ministry. That was probably a good thing for my pride, because I thought I was going to be a good minister, but it was also something I couldn't take too seriously because of other encouragement I had received to move ahead. I think the fact that my local church had confirmed my calling was what strengthened my commitment to go on.

I had been given a place to study theology at Cambridge, so I took it. In my third year, the master of my college asked whether I wanted to take part in an exchange scheme with McGill University in Montreal for two years. It sounded interesting (I did not know anything about Canada then except that there were polar bears and frozen lands). When the master of my college asked, I said, "I'll need to pray about it and ask advice." I asked advice, and on the whole, people said, "Go—it can't do you any harm," which shows a sort of English superiority.

According to my plans, at the end of the two years I would go back to England and do another term in an English theological college to finish off. I knew where I wanted to work—as a curate for somebody I knew. I had it all planned, but God had other ideas. The bishop asked me if I would stay on in Montreal to be a part-time chaplain to students at McGill and to Montreal's Diocesan Theological College and to be a lecturer in liturgy. I felt quite apprehensive about many aspects of this, because—for one—I did not know much about liturgy. Before being ordained I told the ordaining bishop that I did not think I could manage being chaplain to the general student population at McGill. He said, "You're called to do that. You've got to do it. God will guide you and strengthen you to do it." It was with some apprehension that I took on these responsibilities. It turned out that my time as chaplain went to the students at McGill more than to those at the theological college. I did fine; God enabled me to. I may not have been the best chaplain, but I was the best that I could be. Situations that you have not yet experienced, such as being hospital chaplain to the dying, often look terrible beforehand. It is when you are involved in the ministry to that dying person that God does give you grace and strength to minister, if you pray before you go in, trusting that he will give you the words to say and a prayer to pray. The whole business of faith begins with an awareness of God's faithfulness that we are not alone in ministry. Someone has likened it to Jesus being the good shepherd, with us as the sheepdogs. When sheepdogs are not chasing sheep around, one finds them close to the shepherd. I think a priest finds strength in ministry because he or she spends time with the shepherd and feels that peace and strength.

When I was elected to be a bishop I was forty-two and had never been a bishop before. It was a rather frightening prospect in some ways, and yet I believed that God had called me to be the Bishop of Montreal because we had held a twenty-four hour diocesan prayer vigil the weekend before the election, with all the churches praying for the life of the diocese, and particularly praying for God's guidance in the election. In some ways I was not even a good prospect to be elected, because I was English-born, and Canada was moving away from English bishops in favour of real Canadians. I had been in Canada for twenty years, so in some ways I was Canadian, but not a genuine Canadian. I had never been elected to be a Regional Dean or to the Diocesan Council or to General Synod or any of that. I had not climbed any sort of ecclesiastical ladder before becoming bishop. It was a real surprise in some ways, but as I say, I felt that God called me, and that God would enable me, that he would give me the grace to be the bishop—the grace that I did not naturally have—and he did.

Curiously, I was ordained in the days before ACPO, so I never was recommended for training for ordination. I was ordained anyway, and nobody asked me if I had been recommended before I became a bishop. One of the blessings of having been rejected by the advisory board in England is that when I sent candidates to ACPO and they came back having been deferred (although I never sent anybody unless I felt that they *should* be accepted), I was able to say, "Well, I was turned down, too." I was able to have some sympathy and to continue to work with them.

As a bishop I looked for candidates who had, first, a clear sense of calling; second, a real faith—a trust in God rather than just a desire to be an academic; third, people who spent time each day praying that they might be in God's will. All the way through ordained ministry it is important to be in God's will. There are a number of positions that open up along the way, and one has to have that sense of being in God's will, because when we are in God's will we will know God's strengthening grace to do the work. Fourth, I wanted to be assured that a person was growing in holiness, that theirs was not just a faith in the mind, but a faith in the heart that was affecting the whole of his or her life. Fifth, I expected that someone who was feeling called to ordained ministry would be involved in ministry in his or her local parish in one way or another, whether that was participating in the life of the youth group, the Sunday School or involved in liturgy. When you are sharing in the life of the church, going forward into ordained ministry is a continuation of the ministry to which you have already been called by God. Sixth, I wanted to be sure that those seeking ordination read Scripture. When I was fourteen years old in my home church, my rector had me to dinner and gave me a little New Testament and told me to read it and to mark it, and I did. It was so marked! I marked all the verses that I felt were important. The house I grew up in had no electricity, and in the evening when I scrambled up to bed—in the summer months it would stay light until almost 11:00—I read this little New Testament. I cannot read the very litle ones now without glasses, but I am sure that those years of feeding on Scripture were very important for my ministry. I learned that from my grandfather, who lived just a block away. Whenever you went there in the morning, you would see him reading his Bible with his magnifying glass. It was so important to him to read and meditate on it, and I do not know how you can be a priest in the church without having a Bible basis.

I trust that these six points will be of use to all who are considering ordination.

CHAPTER 12

GETTING THE MOST OUT OF SEMINARY

George Sumner and Merv Mercer

Preparation

The first matter to address when thinking about how to get the most out of your time in theological college or seminary is preparation. What should you be doing before you go to seminary? One of the things we hear from bishops periodically is that people's familiarity with the Bible is uneven. For some people, theological college is difficult because the kind of critical study one engages in with regard to the Scriptures presumes that you know the story, that you have a basic familiarity with the data. If you do not, then you are being critical about something you have not first seen in its natural habitat, which is the church. When I went to Yale Divinity School, we had a Bible content test at the end of the first year, and I soon found that there were some stretches of the Book of Chronicles that were new ground for me. Reading Scripture is one important thing you can do in preparation.

Rootedness

The other thing that is important to have is a rootedness in the church from which you are coming. You need to have some kind of home base as you go off to school that includes people who can pray for you. Some students come from a parish they have been in a while and have lots of support; others may not have as much. It is very helpful to have a home base of people who can pray for you; they can give you a point against which you can triangulate with the stars.

If you are currently doing an undergraduate degree at university, it is important to have as broad a background as possible. Some religious studies background is obviously helpful, but the wider you read and the more curious you are about a lot of subjects, the stronger your background will be upon starting formal theological studies.

Spiritual Formation

It might seem a bit outrageous to address the question of what it means to go to seminary or theological college and nurture your spiritual life, because lots of people assume that when you are studying theology, you *are* nurturing your spiritual life. I am here to tell you that it is not necessarily so. One can actually do lots of learning without appropriating that learning in one's heart. Life at a theological college is extremely busy: one book after another, one essay after another—lots of tasks. To complete those tasks successfully and earn a degree is not necessarily the same as growing spiritually. You need to go to seminary with an awareness that your spiritual journey needs to be nurtured at least as much as your intellectual journey, and that your learning in courses needs to be sunk deep into your heart, into your relationship with Christ. That is not actually easy to do.

There is a lot in an academic institution that seems to work against growing spiritually. Students who talk to me often complain, "I feel like I study theology all day. The last thing I want to do at night is open the Bible; I mean isn't it all the same?" In fact it is not—growing spiritually is not the same as learning theology. Of course it can be, but you have to actually work at that to make it successful. In a very diverse ecumenical setting such as ours, some professors manage to do what they do without, apparently, much particular faith. They do it as technicians, not necessarily out of a sense of Christ's calling on their lives. It may start that way, but it may not finish that way. Thankfully, that is not always the case; nevertheless, it is something you encounter. Therefore part of your agenda is to make your spiritual growth vital and important.

There are lots of resources to assist you with this goal, including the previously mentioned example about a group of people whom you can call your home base. All of you should have a fan club, people who have affirmed your calling, who know you intimately and well—maybe a group of two or three with whom you can enter a covenant. You need people for whom your prayer support is a commitment and to whom you will tell your needs. These should be people totally outside the seminary—a group who will covenant to work with you and who will keep you connected with your roots, your home parish.

You will get more out of your seminary experience, I believe, if you are prepared for major adjustments in your spiritual life. Do not be naive about what it means to come into a new setting. You will have some sense of dislocation, and you will have to develop new patterns, especially in your spiritual life. Often students say, "You know, I just don't know where my God fits in this new setting," and it takes time to develop that. It is better to be prepared for it rather than being bitter, six weeks in, that no one seems to talk about God the way you talk about God. Be prepared for this sense of adjustment; realize that people have diverse expressions for their faith, that worship is diverse from place to place, and that you are going to have to have some flexibility. To be forewarned is to be forearmed.

With all of the biblical studies undertaken in a Master of Divinity program, one would think that knowing more Scripture would translate to more devotion. It is not necessarily so. If you have not done so already, develop ways in which Scripture is part of your devotional life—the simple activity of reading Scripture and hearing God's voice rather than trying to analyse or figure out what it might mean. Listening to God's tender voice to you is not covered in your courses; it is something you have to maintain and develop for yourself.

At Wycliffe College, we have started a program of spiritual mentors. The College undertakes to provide—external to the academic world of the College—a team of a dozen spiritual mentors whom we pay to walk with our students through their theological education. Each student has the opportunity to select one of the mentors with whom to discuss his or her faith journey in a one-to-one relationship on a monthly basis. Students have really appreciated this. It has taken a long time for the Protestant schools to realize that mentorship is an important and vital part of what it means to grow spiritually. There are lots of things that you may not want to talk to a professor about— just as a cleric might not want to talk to the bishop about his or her struggles, so a theological student does not always want to talk to the professor of theology about where his or her doubts are. The spiritual mentor is someone who can pray with you through your struggles, someone who will hold you accountable to the journey upon which you have embarked. Spiritual mentorship is a tremendous resource, and it is our hope that you will develop it as a life-long habit. Even those who are leading in the church need someone with whom to reflect on a deep faith level.

Part of your spiritual life is worship. I do not know why it is so hard to get seminarians to come to church. One would think that they just long for worship. If you go into seminary having made a covenant with yourself to participate, consistently and actively, in the worship life, it will pay dividends for you. You will maximize the learning that you are undergoing in your courses. Even at the end of term, when the essays begin to mount up, and every minute feels precious, and you are thinking, "No one's taking attendance, maybe I'll just not go, I'll grab a quick supper, and get that essay done," I would encourage you to hold fast to your commitment to yourself to participate in the worship life. Anytime you talk about spiritual nurture, you had better be ready for God's surprises. God will surprise you, and his surprises will blow you away again and again throughout the three years. Be ready, because that is part of getting the most out of your seminary experience, and it is part of your spiritual life.

Inquiry

When I went to theological college I was a cradle Anglican. I'd had an experience of conversion in college, from which arose the question of ordination. I took a year off and wrestled with that question. I was motivated spiritually, yet intellectually my exposure to the church was limited. The first year of theological college was like going into a mine and finding vast treasures. Intellectually, the Christian tradition was something deeper and more ancient and more coherent than I had imagined. A Jewish theologian named Franz Rosenschweig had a similar experience to mine. He was a secular Jew in the early part of the twentieth century. Out of curiosity he went into a synagogue on the Jewish Day of Atonement and had an experience of having his whole foundation shaken. He encountered something which was much more vast and imposing, both theologically and spiritually, than he had reckoned. In a Christian mode, my experience was somewhat similar: seminary was the beginning of a conversation with the great Christian minds. I discovered how very relevant Augustine and the church fathers were—as great voices addressing the perennial questions that were my questions. Nurture a sense of openness and desire a deep engagement with the tradition. The tradition has its struggles, but you need to enter into the great debates that have shaped our faith.

Since I began with a Jewish example, I'll describe the second aspect of inquiry as *chutzpah*—by which I mean nerve. I must admit I was not very good at this. I was a little daunted by my professors and did not go to ask them questions in their office hours. I should have. You must have the nerve to assume that the big questions you have are the perennial questions that they are wrestling with as well. Ask in class, then go to talk to them. Professors are delighted to have people come talk to them about what they have said. Ask questions like, "How do human beings actually exercise their will?" "How are they free and yet God is utterly sovereign?" Theology wrestles with just such questions.

The third important aspect of inquiry is to make a distinction (theology is making distinctions) between internal critique and external critique. Theology, in all its different branches, is, as St. Anselm says, "faith seeking understanding." That is, it moves from faith; it assumes faith; the challenges it offers to you are within the context of faith. In other words, the appropriate theological challenge assumes the truth of the creed, and then it asks all kinds of questions: How do the pieces fit together? How does that fit together with some of the assumptions we make in the modern world, and what about those assumptions? There can be lots of questioning and struggle within the context of faith. The assumption is that since God is all truth, we have nothing to fear from this struggle—as long as it is within the context of faith.

Personal Characteristics

The following list of personal traits is by no means universal, but it represents some things that come to mind as important.

First, if you come to seminary in a suit of armour, you will not get the most out of it—so you need to come with a sense of openness. You will find new communities of faith, new experiences of ministry, and if you are open to them, you will learn from them, and it will enhance your experience. So many evangelicals seem to come to seminary with a metallic, clanking kind of step. It is very hard, I think, to make the most of a seminary experience if you come to it with a closed mind. For example, every other year, we take a group of students to Kenya. Those students come back transformed and changed by the experience of going to a completely different Anglican Christian community in Kenya. That is one of the ways that a richness can be received. If you are closed, you do not receive it, so that sense of openness is really important. Vulnerability—a willingness to be vulnerable and to risk—is also important. We are greedy here at a theological college. We want everyone to offer their gifts, because they inform and enhance and enrich the communal life. Be willing to step up to the plate and say, "Here I am, and this is what I do, and some people have found this helpful, and I want you to know about it, and I want it to take its place," because that is how our community is formed every year. In fact, every year it is re-formed because of new people who have come and old ones who have left. Be prepared to say, "This is who I am. Enjoy me and accept me." I have to say that this is easier for an extrovert than for an introvert. I am a deep introvert—I would be happier under the table than talking to you! However, even an introvert should nurture the sense of making the most of the community and being as integrated into it as possible.

The second characteristic is a hard one to cultivate, but it is important—and that is to make critique and assessment a friend as you discern who you are becoming in ministry. As you engage the possibility of being ordained in the church you will encounter critique and assessment—and you will also encounter it in theological college. Sometimes people resist this, feel uncomfortable with it or do not know how to deal with a particular critique. The more you are able to make critique the grist for your mill of growth, the more you will get out of your seminary experience. Actually, critique of your weaknesses comes hand in hand with assessment of your strengths. You will receive affirmations and you will be encouraged to grow in certain ways. Critique has two faces, and you need both of them. If you come to seminary anxious about what people might say about you, you will not get the most out of your experience. In other words, stand confidently in the fact that God has brought you to this place and let that confidence overpower any sense of threat you might feel about being assessed and evaluated. I look out on a class every day and think, "These are people God has brought to this place to learn more about himself." May I perish if I do not value that and cherish that. The situation is no different than some future Sunday morning when you will stand up in front of people after a particularly difficult advisory board meeting, committee meeting or warden's meeting in which some feelings were hurt, and you will probably think, "Gosh, I don't know if I want to stand in front of this community alone today." But you need to know that God has invited them to be there that day. "Love them for my sake," he has said. You will have the sense, sometimes, of being assaulted on all sides. There will be times when you need to remind yourself that you are in a particular place because God has called you and brought you there. Live confidently in that understanding.

One of the things that happens in theological education sometimes is that each of the disciplines—biblical studies, theology, pastoral theology and church history—develop their own vocabulary and language, and the further into each of them you go, the more separate they seem to be, the more discreet their syntax. Your job is actually to make connections between them; they all interrelate, especially if you are in parish leadership. I have yet to see a problem in parish leadership that was only a theological problem or only a historical problem. Seminaries are doing their best to develop courses that are interdisciplinary, because you need to be "integrated" when you come out into the church in order to be able to take all of the resources that you have been given in your education and bring them to bear on the challenges in ministry. Make connections. That is something you will be helped with, but it is also something to which you must be alert.

You must also begin to lead a balanced life. There are a lot of clergy who do not have a balanced life and often they have learned their imbalance in theological college. People called to leadership are often "type A" personalities of some sort—they are driven, they are doers. I want to say, "*being* matters"—and this is what the spiritual life is about. Therefore, think about playing hard and praying hard as well as studying hard. A balanced life is something to seek out—even at the end of term when it looks like you will never get finished. You always get finished. The work always gets done.

Finally, celebrate the growth that will happen in you. Remember that growth always involves change, and if you are afraid of change, you will not get the most out of your seminary experience. Celebrate growth and embrace change.

The Church

First of all, it is important to recognize that theological colleges exist in the interstitial zone—between the university (the academic world) and the church (the public arena). There is some space between theological colleges and the church, but they are related, and they look somewhat similar. The church is changing—certainly the emphasis on lay ministry is important today—and theological college has come to reflect those changes. Most schools will have some people who are there because they want to learn more about God, some people who are there to become professional lay ministers, some people who want to be ordained, some who want to go on to doctoral study and maybe some who are in doctoral study. Each school will be a slightly different mix. If you go to theological college and are not yet sure whether you are on the way to ordination or perhaps a professional lay ministry, that is hardly unique. One of the keys to the community is to get all the components to act synergistically, to work together. The sense that people who are there for different purposes, yet all within one community, all with the goal of worshipping God with their hearts and minds, ought to make that community stronger.

Theological colleges also resemble the church in that the ages of people who are attending vary widely. I recently talked to a person in Halifax who said, "I'm forty. I wonder if I'm going to be the oldest person there." I said, "Think again. Not even close." The age diversity is great. People are coming from various situations in their lives: second careers, third careers or straight out of college, for example. Whoever you are, there are going to be other folks like you there. That is a good thing, but it is also a challenge to theological colleges. One of the challenges is that the appropriate way to engage in theological education is sometimes different for people who are coming from a second career, with a lot of experience, than for those who are straight out of college. Both groups are there, and it is incumbent on the schools to provide an education that works for a very wide spectrum.

Now this may seem obvious, but I think it is worth saying that "orders" are orders *in and for the church.* On the other hand, one wants to have some desire to be part of the renewal of the church. But there has to be a sense of love for the church and a desire to serve the church—and to serve God through the church, of course. It is important because one can sometimes start to feel either alienated from or separated from the church. There is a lot in the church that needs renewing, but one has to bear in mind that ordained ministry is the ordering of the church. It is so important to meet people who are ordained and are admirable examples of living faithfully, honestly and loyally within the church. At its best, field ministry can provide this opportunity as can spiritual mentoring. One of the things I really enjoy about being the principal of Wycliffe College is meeting and talking with some of the older alumni—people who graduated in the 1930s who are warriors and have been through a lot. Many of them have emerged from their years of ministry with a triumphant spirit, and they are just wonderful people to be around. Being with them is tremendously encouraging and renewing to me as a priest, because they have realistic pastoral experience in the church that has not rendered them cynical, but has deepened their spiritual lives. It can and should happen at theological college; it should happen within ordained ministry as well.

CHAPTER 13

MINISTRY TO FIRST NATIONS COMMUNITIES

Christopher Williams and Lydia Constant

Bishop Chris Williams

What follows are the ideas that Lydia and I would like to share with you about ministry to First Nations communities. You will get two entirely different perspectives, and that is as it should be, because the first mistake so many interested people make, I think, is to consider all First Nations people the same. They are not. First Nations people think all non-First Nations people are the same, and of course they are not either. We will begin with my point of view, which is that of someone who is not a First Nations person, but who has worked among the First Nations people for forty years. However, I know that I will never have the same mindset as the people to whom I have tried to minister.

I have spent forty years in the Diocese of the Arctic. It is the only ministry I have ever known. My story began when I went to my theological college, which was St. John's College, Durham in England. I first visited as a postulant to be interviewed by the principal to see whether or not he was willing to accept me. He was not expecting me, and so I was handed over to the college chaplain, who opened the door of the common room, and there was one man standing there reading the paper. The chaplain said, "Here, take care of this young man. Bring him to supper, and the principal will see him afterwards." So I went up to this man's room. As I wandered around his room, I saw on the mantle a little piece of ceramic, and it was in the shape of an igloo. I went over to it, picked it up and said, "What is this?" Now, depending on your viewpoint, that was either the stupidest or the most meaningful question I ever asked in my life—because that was when I first heard about the ministry of the church in the Arctic. That particular student never did go to the Arctic, but somehow his mantle fell upon me, so that at the end of my time in college I felt that I could not accept a position in England without first testing my vocation to go to the north. The Bishop of the Arctic offered me a position, and the rest is history.

We are the largest diocese in the Anglican Communion, just a matter of about three-and-a-quarter-million square miles. We stretch from the Yukon Territories/Alaska border to the Atlantic Ocean. We stretch from the North Pole down severally to the top of the provinces, and indeed in the province of Quebec, down towards the bottom of James Bay. At times we have been asked to have jurisdiction at the North Pole; my predecessor was asked by one of his clergy for permission to conduct a wedding at the North Pole, although permission was not given. Of our congregations, three are what I would call non-native congregations, and three are mixed. The other twenty-five congregations in the diocese are predominantly First Nations people, and even more predominantly Inuit, or Eskimo. For a number of years, since 1970, we have had our own college for training Inuit ordinands, called the Arthur Turner Training School, Pangnirtung. That college has a principal who oversees the running of the college and does some of the teaching. We have been blessed over the years by having men and women come—from all over the world, in fact—to teach a certain part of each of the courses. I am looking forward now to next fall, when George Sumner has consented to come and be one of our visiting lecturers. As a result of the work of that college, we now have seventeen clergy in the diocese who are Inuit, compared with twelve who are non-Inuit. We have two Inuit bishops, including Bishop Paul Idlout, who was the first Inuit bishop of the Anglican Church. Our Synod is overwhelmingly Inuit, with some people from the Dene tribes of the western Arctic.

Our policy over the years has been to build up indigenous ministry, both stipendiary and non-stipendiary. This has happened mainly, but not exclusively, in our First Nations parishes. Your first question, I am sure, could be, "Well, then, if you're going towards an indigenous ministry, where do I fit in? Is there still a ministry for the southern, non-native, maybe seminary-trained clergyperson?" The answer is most definitely "Yes," but perhaps not in a traditional sense. We have fifty-one congregations that are grouped into thirty parishes. Because of the way our diocese is so scattered, because of financial restraints and especially because of the high cost of travel, we are turning more and more to locally raised and trained non-stipendiary clergy. What we need, then, are men and women willing to go north, but willing to go in the context of what is now called "mutual ministry"—not as I did, to pastor a congregation, but to be those who will oversee, inspire, encourage and train locally raised-up clergy. (There is what I often call "the case of the misplaced comma," which you may know of, in the epistle to the Ephesians. In the days of the King James Version, in Ephesians 4:11–12, Paul lays out the "charisms" of the church, saying, "It was he [Christ, the one who ascended] who gave some to be apostles, some to be prophets, some to be evangelists, and some to be pastors and teachers, to prepare God's people for the work of service." In the Authorized Version, there did not used to be an extra comma before the last phrase, as if the "works of service" was just another of these ministries within the church.)

I think now we have it straight: the purpose of the ordained ministry, as I see it, is not to do for people what they can do for themselves, but to enable them to do that ministry which is theirs. I was very impressed with one of my congregations when I visited as bishop. We had a wonderful service, taken from the *Book of Alternative Services*—this was one of the occasions when several services can be combined. It was essentially a confirmation service, but in that confirmation service we had an adult baptism, an infant baptism, one being received into the church from another denomination, others who wanted to renew their baptismal vows in a special way, a group of teenage confirmees and another group of what I would call adult confirmees. When the time came for each of these groups to be presented to the bishop, they were each presented by a different member of the congregation, who had been responsible for preparing them for that day, under the overall oversight of the parish priest. The priest had enabled the congregation members; they had, in turn, enabled these candidates. I thought it was a wonderful and truly practical understanding of the work of the church.

What are the challenges, then—or, I would prefer to say, the opportunities—in northern ministry, in First Nations ministry? The first thing to understand is that we do not want three-month experts. There is a saying in the north that after three months, one knows everything there is to know; it is only after three years—or maybe thirty years—in the north that one finds out how much one does not know. The first challenge that anyone going into First Nations ministry from the outside will have to face is gaining the respect and the acceptance of their congregation—and that does not come quickly. The bishop under whom I first worked in the north, Bishop Donald Marsh, used to say, "In the first five years [and in those days, our term of service was five years] you learn to know your congregation. In the second five years you can begin to achieve something." If you are not prepared to stay for the second five years, there is really no point in going for the first. I do not mean to pin it down to specific lengths of time, but what the First Nations ministry needs is people who are willing to make a long-term commitment to it—not, as so often happens, to make it a stepping-stone, something to do to serve out your apprenticeship after leaving college and before passing on to something else.

One of our first-year duties in going to the north was made very clear to us: it was to learn to the language, that which is the instrument of culture. You learn a people's culture as you learn their language. People realize that you are showing respect for them, even as you stumble and stutter and struggle to speak their language, because it shows them that you are willing to meet them on their ground—instead of expecting the opposite, as many non-native people do. In many parts of the north, and I think throughout the native ministry of our church now, we realize that English is widely spoken, especially by young adults and youth. However it is still a fact in our diocese that in all but six of our congregations, the major service, on any given Sunday, is in some language other than English. Therefore I would ask anyone coming into the north that they be willing to make at least an *attempt* to be liturgically proficient, wherever that is necessary. In other words, we must be willing to join people in worship in their own language.

Another challenge for many people is that of hardship. We are not a people that like hardship. You know what they say: "When the going gets tough," most of us decide it is time to get going. Working with native people, in the north especially, there is the challenge of isolation—not just for the minister, but also for the minister's family and children. There is also a high cost of living, and unfortunately those in First Nations ministry in our country are paid on a minimum stipend. There are primitive conditions. When I first went north, in my first parish, we got mail delivery once a year when the boat came in! We also had the benefit of an airdrop from the Canadian Air Force—an extra delivery of Christmas mail. My first Christmas, my parents sent me a package. Being traditional, I was determined not to open it until Christmas day, but I could not resist looking at the customs label, and there it was: one dinner service—from

10,000 feet, by parachute! In certain areas I am finding that it is not possible now even to place married couples with older children. One of our ministers had done faithful service in the north, but he had a fourteen-year-old daughter, and she was the only person in her class in school who was not sexually active. He thought that for the sake of his family it was necessary to leave.

What type of people are we looking for? First and foremost, of course, it must be those who are called by God. If God is not calling you to this ministry, you will not last. If you are not there because God wants you to be there, then it would be better for you to be somewhere else.

We need people who are self-reliant. I come down south and I hear clergy complaining that they have to go to yet another clergy clericus—that they had one last month and now they are having another one. I would give my right arm if we could call our clergy together even once a year. We need those of you who are self-starters, because you will not have the Archdeacon on your back finding out what you are doing. You will be out there largely by yourself for a good part of the year. If you cannot get yourself up in the morning and start your ministry, nobody else will be around to do it for you.

We need, obviously, people who are grounded in their faith and in the gospel, people who are not just preaching the Word but living the Word, because our First Nations communities are very close, very intimate. My wife went to a missionary training college in London, England many years ago. It was a ladies' training college for women going overseas to China and India and many other places. At this college you were never allowed to go for a walk by yourself, because it was thought that when you went out into the mission field you would never be alone; you would always have people constantly around you, constantly watching you, constantly seeing what you were up to. You can preach all you like in the pulpit, but if your life does not show what you preach, then your ministry will come to naught.

We need people who are adaptable and flexible. After all, you are ministering to people who are not your own, people whose ways are not your ways. Many things that they do will seem strange; many of their values will seem strange to you. On the other hand, many of them will also be wonderful teachers from whom you can learn much. I shiver sometimes when I think of some of the things I did in my first years in the north, but I also give thanks for some of the things that I learned. I remember on one occasion I was getting very agitated about a certain man in the congregation, and my catechist at that time came to me and said, "Why are you getting so mad at so-and-so?" I said, "Because he's committing adultery, and adultery is a sin!" My catechist turned to me and said, "Yes! But you are equally a sinner!" I replied, "What do you mean?" He said, "You're getting angry, and anger is just as much a sin as adultery." Ever since that time, I have found it very hard to be judgmental. You know the old saying, that if you point your finger at somebody, you have three fingers pointing back at yourself?

We need people who are practical, because in the north, if a thing needs doing, you do it yourself. I remember one time my bishop had some money and decided that he was going to put water systems in all the mission houses. He sent me this letter and gave me the details and said, "Here you are. I'm sending you this water system—hot and cold running water for the whole house!" I said, "But who's going to install it?" He replied, "You are!" Luckily there was a plumber in the community for a couple of days. He taught me how to sweat copper joints together, and eventually the water system was complete. Therefore we need people who are not only good scholars, but who are also very practical and can repair things; people who can take nothing and make something from it.

What are the rewards? Adventure! The north is still a place of adventure, a place of great beauty, a place of variety in ministry. I can guarantee you will never be bored with it. Before I went to the north people were giving me books and things, saying, "Here you are. This will help to pass the long winter nights." I still have the books, because I never found the long winter nights! There is always such a variety of ministry to occupy you and challenge you. I believe that ministry in the north is an opportunity to be on the cutting edge of our church's work. In particular, I believe that the northern ministry is on the leading edge of the church's work of evangelism. I am the Episcopal visitor in the summer to an organization that you may know—it is a short-term missions organization working mainly overseas. For a century, missionaries have been coming from southern Canada and from England into the north with the gospel. Now for the first time, in the fall there will be a team of Inuit clergy and lay people coming down to conduct missions in the Diocese of Toronto! That, to me, represents the wheel having come full circle.

Northern ministry is a challenge, but it is an opportunity and a privilege to work with some of the most wonderful (though sometimes some of the most frustrating) people in the world. It is an opportunity to see them grow in faith and in the knowledge of our Lord Jesus. We should also remember that there are probably more indigenous people now living in southern Canada than all those who live in the northern part of the provinces. Vancouver has its own community of indigenous people, as do most of the major centres—principally places like Calgary, Edmonton, Winnipeg, Toronto and Montreal. Therefore the challenges of ministry to First Nations people are great. We still need the expertise and the gifts of those who come from the south very much in our northern ministry. We need these so that the northern people themselves, the indigenous people, can take their stand fully and equally in the life of the church.

Archdeacon Lydia Constant

I will be sharing my experiences in the form of a report on how the development of ministry is currently being conducted in our First Nations communities. I am from the Ojibwe Nation, and I speak the Swampee Cree language. English is my second language. I was ordained in 1988 and priested in 1990. I do not have a parish of my own—since I became an archdeacon, I have been able to travel around the surrounding communities. As Chris has said, in some places they do not have an Archdeacon behind them, but I have the privilege of being right behind all of the priests in our deanery. I also work at the Henry Budd College for Ministry. I have been there for ten years now, and I have been very involved in that ministry, including the hospital chaplaincy. I was born in that hospital, and I haven't made a move yet! I am also the mother of three children and am blessed with six grandchildren.

You probably wonder why I am an ordained person. I became a widow when my husband passed away in 1984—actually, he committed suicide. I came that close to going with him, because he missed me a couple of times with his shotgun. That same year I encountered God's calling. My husband passed away in January; I entered the college in September. After the funeral I was sitting in my bedroom, kind of listening and thinking, with many things going through my mind. Then all of a sudden I visualized a window being opened in front of me. From that windowsill I could see a straight road, and the road looked eternal, with no ending. I felt some kind of presence, or warmth—and yet, at the same time, a feeling of hardship. I knew then that I had to take that road. And now I know what that road meant. There are so many things that I have encountered in my ministry. Being a woman, there are so many times I have been rejected; there are so many hard roads to travel among the native communities. When you try to deal with your own kind, it is not easy; you are rejected even though you are the same. However, what is important is the ministry to which God is calling you. For example, despite all the residential school damage, a voice was heard, and that was a turning point in the church. That was where the indigenous people—on a national level and on a local level—found their voice and the strength to become the Anglican Council of Indigenous Peoples. In 1994 the covenant was established—the covenant that reads, "Under the guidance of the God-Spirit we agree to do all we can to call our people into a unity and a self-determining community within the Anglican Church of Canada. To this end we extend a hand of partnership to all who will help us build a truly indigenous Anglican Church in Canada. May God bless this new vision and give us grace to accomplish it." The newly introduced covenant, which was reaffirmed at the gathering, offers a way for all Anglicans to join in a new partnership in the gospel. The indigenous church is not seeking separation but self-determination: walking side by side without domination, listening to one another and learning from one another both at the national level and at the diocesan level. That wish has now been heard many times, and it has been the subject of dialogue all across Canada.

Now I want to talk about my work with the Henry Budd College for Ministry. Henry Budd was the first Canadian Indian to be ordained as an Anglican priest. The college named for him was founded in 1980. It came into being on the initiative of the Diocese of Brandon in response to the expressed need for indigenous people in leadership and as a result of the growing interest in training for indigenous ministry. The purpose of the Henry Budd College is to equip indigenous people for ministry within the church. The college continues to provide ministry development and to move indigenous people into the roles of deacons and priests in each community.

The first thing that we do in the college is lay training. Students enroll in introductory Bible courses based on general interest. They choose their programs, keeping in mind that they could be eligible for a lay certificate issued by Cook School, the school offering theological education by extension. The college believes that every student can learn. That means that we travel to each community and offer these courses, this program at their level. Most of our students have only completed Grade Two, Grade Five or Grade Eight. Seldom do we have someone with a Grade Twelve education. The next step is the advanced lay ministry program, which is thirty credits. (In our program one credit represents approximately ten hours of time spent in class, plus the necessary preparation time.) It is a more specialized version of the lay ministry program, which prepares students for volunteer lay ministry. Students who have completed the thirty credits to earn the advanced lay leadership certificate may be offered as possible candidates for ordination. The educational experiences

MINISTRY TO FIRST NATIONS COMMUNITIES

provided in this program are broader than what can be provided in the various communities.

Candidates then undergo ordination training: they have to experience fieldwork, completing at least twelve weeks of supervised ministry. I was one of the students that went to Winnipeg to do my clinical pastoral education, but most of our students are doing their fieldwork within local hospitals, jail ministries and senior citizens' homes. In most cases the Henry Budd students are expected to be ordained part way through their training so that further preparation can happen on the job. Although more students are training for lay ministry, the original intention was always to prepare indigenous people for ordained, stipendiary ministry in their own communities.

We realize that ministry is not a job, but an obligation and a duty required by God. In our selection process we go into the communities to consult people about a particular candidate. We ask for parish recommendations so that we can ask questions about this particular person of members of their own parishes. Many of the referees will say, "We have known this person ever since he was born." Because they know this person through and through, they will provide recommendations about the training that this particular person should go through. We then organize an ACPO committee, usually made up of our own people, so that mostly native assessors assess candidates. The bishop will also receive input from all examining chaplains before making a final decision about ordination in each individual case. The candidates will continue to undergo training with the lay people, the students that are learning to grow in their spirituality. We kind of mix them all together so that they have this special experience before and after ordination. After they are ordained they still continue to be supervised in a supportive manner.

Recently I attended a conference in Winnipeg. At the national level, we are "getting ready." What is the future of the church? What is our future? We have made a covenant for the benefit of the whole church, the church of the future. We envision that this church will be grounded in the Holy Scripture and in God's grace. Its foundation will be forgiveness, which is a core value for indigenous people, based on our traditional and our biblical teachings. In the church of the future all peoples will be treated with respect, as equals, and all voices will be heard. For the new candidates that are thinking about working with the native peoples, we welcome you. Yes, you can work with us. Yes, you can walk beside us, you can pray with us, you can continue to train with us, you can share our hurts, and we will share your hurts. Sharing hurts is the road of healing. And this is the road our indigenous peoples are travelling. We are suffering, and we realize the church is suffering, too, because we are the church. That is why we need a lot of healing, a lot of help—so that we can journey together in this life.

www.ingramcontent.com/pod-product-compliance
Lightning Source LLC
Chambersburg PA
CBHW022022090426
42739CB00006BA/248